Emergency State

Emergency State

How We Lost Our Freedoms in the Pandemic and Why It Matters

ADAM WAGNER

THE BODLEY HEAD
LONDON

1 3 5 7 9 10 8 6 4 2

The Bodley Head is part of the Penguin Random House group of companies
whose addresses can be found at global.penguinrandomhouse.com

First published by The Bodley Head in 2022

Graph and timeline designed by Jason Mitchell, Argo Creative Limited

penguin.co.uk/vintage

Typeset in 12/14.75pt Bembo MT Pro by Jouve (UK), Milton Keynes.
Printed and bound in Great Britain by Clays Ltd, Elcograf S.p.A.

The authorised representative in the EEA is Penguin Random House Ireland,
Morrison Chambers, 32 Nassau Street, Dublin D02 YH68

A CIP catalogue record for this book is available from the British Library

ISBN 9781847927460

Penguin Random House is committed to a sustainable
future for our business, our readers and our planet. This book
is made from Forest Stewardship Council® certified paper.

To Julia, Joseph, Miri and Bonnie,
and to my parents, Alison and Anthony

Contents

Preface

'From this evening I must give the British people a very simple instruction – you must stay at home.'

On Monday 23 March 2020, shortly after 8:30 p.m., Boris Johnson broadcast these eighteen startling words to the nation.[1] For the first time in the country's history, a twenty-four-hour curfew was imposed upon the population. All 'non-essential' businesses would be shut. Schools closed. Families divided. Group worship banned. Life as we knew it replaced by a new reality, where our singular focus would be to slow the spread of a deadly new virus, COVID-19.

For the millions watching, the new reality the Prime Minister was imposing was hard enough to digest. The lockdown which had seemed so far away, which the government had suggested just days before would not happen here, was suddenly a reality. But the shock of the new reality was accompanied by another huge shift for our society. Not only was the lockdown rearranging the basic reality of our social lives, it would also create a new legal universe. For the next two years, the tiniest details of our lives – from whether we could leave the house, where we could work, even whom we could *hug* – would be decreed by ministers, controlled by strange new laws the likes of which had no precedent in living memory and enforced by what often resembled a police state.

In his statement, the Prime Minister called COVID-19 the 'invisible killer'. But something else was invisible that spring evening – the law which was to back up his unprecedented instruction. He had stated that there were four limited purposes for which people would be allowed to leave home, and if they did not follow the rules 'the police will have the powers to enforce them'. But no such powers existed. This was no small detail. It meant we did not know, as the country was thrust into the lockdown, the legal basis for the police powers, what kind of enforcement and penalties would be meted out to lockdown breachers – and most importantly, we did not know exactly what the rules *were*. The Prime Minister's statement was bracing but vague, mentioning people could leave their homes to shop only for 'basic necessities', to take 'one form of exercise per day', to provide care for a 'vulnerable person' or travel to and from work if it was 'absolutely necessary and cannot be done from home'. This was not sufficiently clear for people to know whether they were breaking the law. As a human rights lawyer, this lack of certainty over the sudden dismantling of basic freedoms rang the loudest of alarm bells.

So, where was the law? I asked the question on Twitter and was given various answers. It could come through the Civil Contingencies Act 2004, an act of Parliament designed to grant sweeping powers in times of 'emergency', defined as an event or situation which threatens serious damage to human welfare or to the environment of a place, or war or terrorism threatening serious damage to security of the United Kingdom.[2] Perhaps the rules would be in the Coronavirus Bill, a vast collection of powers and rules which was being rushed through Parliament at breakneck speed even as the Prime Minister stood up to address the nation. Or maybe through an obscure public health statute which had provided the basis for the law which – at the stroke of a ministerial pen – closed non-essential businesses two days earlier.[3] It was like a legal murder mystery. Which law would be used to remove our freedoms?

The answer was that the law did not yet exist. It would not appear until three days later, posted on a government website at around 3 p.m. on Thursday 26 March.[4] In eleven short pages, the new regulations would lock down tens of millions of people, forcing them to stay at home, banning public gatherings, giving police powers to use reasonable force to disperse gatherings and take people back to their homes, and creating criminal offences to punish people if they were caught breaching the new rules. Fixed Penalty Notices (FPNs) would offer the opportunity to avoid criminal prosecution by paying a penalty of between £100 for a first offence and £960 for a third. By March 2022, two years later, over 100,000 FPNs would have been issued,[5] including, most notoriously, to the Prime Minister himself, along with 125 other officials at the heart of government. Almost 2,000 people would be prosecuted for offences under the regulations, including people who were protesting the regulations themselves, and many whose cases were heard in private hearings from which the public and press were barred.[6]

Since the lockdown law restricted our rights more than any other in history, you might have expected such a bonfire of liberties to be fiercely debated in Parliament before becoming law. But it was not debated at all. Using an emergency procedure, the law came into force the moment it was signed by the Health Secretary, Matt Hancock. Hancock utilised what turned out to be almost unimaginably vast powers under the Public Health (Control of Disease) Act 1984. This act of Parliament had last been in the public eye when the Thatcher government used it to detain infected people during the AIDS epidemic. But since those days, the 1984 Act had been quietly upgraded – *turbocharged* – meaning it could now be used not just to detain individuals but to place millions under effective house arrest. And, with huge implications for our democracy, these powers could be used without Parliament having any say until weeks later. When Parliament was finally able to vote on the powers, the vote would be a simple yes or no, with no opportunity to amend the law.

It is important properly to set the scene for any criticism of what happened to our laws, constitution and democracy by remembering what it felt like to be facing a swiftly emerging social catastrophe. The country, and the world, were confronted by a true emergency, one long foretold but not experienced for a century. A pandemic which, according to the World Health Organization, killed almost 15 million people worldwide in its first two years,[7] and over 200,000 in the UK, including tens of thousands in care homes during the first wave.[8] It is therefore possible to excuse a lot of what happened in those frantic, at times terrifying, early weeks of the COVID-19 pandemic.

But worrying aspects of those first few weeks – the disconnect between what politicians announced and what the law said, mass confusion caused by unclear laws, the downgrading of Parliament to a glorified rubber stamp, the basic lack of accountability and scrutiny of those making vastly restrictive laws – would become a pattern lasting *two years*, and even beyond. As we faced two years of severe restrictions on our freedoms, these issues would rear their heads again and again, corroding our democratic institutions and our trust in the government's ability to act fairly and without corruption.

Nothing remotely like this has happened before in the UK. The Second World War saw huge restrictions on civilian life, but in many respects this went further. Government decisions with vast implications for our lives were taken at speed, some of which are still being felt today. Events also happened at massive scale and with breathless pace, from lockdowns to variants to hotel quarantine to Partygate. The UK's constitution is not written down in one place, but it is uncontroversial to say that Parliament is at its centre. Only a handful of the laws were meaningfully debated in Parliament, and just nine were considered *before* they came into force. With the government lurching from crisis to crisis, and new laws appearing on an almost daily basis, it was almost impossible to keep up with, let alone keep track of, the constitutional damage being done.

But I kept the receipts. For over a decade I have worked to make human rights law accessible, to explain the law and comment on legal developments through social media, blogs, podcasts and a charity I set up. At the same time, I act in prominent court cases involving human rights abuses. As the pandemic began, it seemed like the different aspects of my work were suddenly aligning, as new laws appeared almost on a daily basis, restricting rights on an extraordinary scale. Over one hundred emergency laws were passed to restrict our lives, roughly one per week on average. I created a table to keep a tally of the ever-changing coronavirus laws.[9] As the government's own efforts were causing so much confusion, I decided to put it online. It developed into an essential resource which included links to my Twitter threads on the changes, threads which were, as events moved on, being read by millions of people. Unexpectedly, my somewhat geeky table also took on a political significance when, in late 2021 and early 2022, I used it to explain how government officials had broken their own laws when holding lockdown-breaching parties behind the doors of Downing Street.

The purpose of this book is to tell the story of the pandemic through the extraordinary restrictions on our freedoms, which made criminal offences of socialising, worshipping, singing, dancing, exercising, even having sex – the most basic activity of our human existence. I will explain how the strange and unprecedented lockdown laws were made and why we need to worry about the implications of the government exercising such enormous power for over two years.

What I will not do is tell you whether every aspect of the restrictions was justified. These are issues of vital importance.

But they are not ones on which a lawyer has the expertise to reach a conclusion. In truth, I doubt we have reached a stage when some judgements can even be made. As I write, the pandemic is still raging, with thousands of cases and deaths per day worldwide. There will be authoritative analyses of which measures 'worked' and which did not, but this book will not provide one – although I will comment on whether it was possible to avoid certain severe restrictions on our freedoms.

I will mostly focus on what happened in England, and in the Westminster government, because to also discuss what happened in Northern Ireland, Scotland and Wales would be too broad a scope for me to manage.

What I will do is tell the story of 763 days, from 14 February 2020, when Matt Hancock made an emergency declaration that COVID-19 constituted a serious and imminent threat to public health, to 18 March 2022, when the latest regulation made under a state of emergency was revoked. During that period of over two years, ministers used the state of emergency to create laws which would control every element of our lives. Within a short period, the state of emergency became an Emergency State, showing aspects of an authoritarianism alien to our way of life and history which many, including myself, would have thought impossible before this crisis began.

It is tempting to put the first two years of the pandemic behind us, to move on from COVID-19 and focus on other important issues, to assume that world events left us with little choice but to shut down society and hand immense power to a small group in government. That temptation is understandable, not least because it is painful to revisit a genuinely traumatic time in our recent history. But it would be a mistake to gloss over what happened in those 763 days, as the state was turned upside down and freedoms we thought untouchable were torn away with hardly a whimper. It is vitally important that we understand how that Emergency State was created – in significant part through accident rather than design, and certainly without being predicted or planned – how the lack of accountability and democratic process led to errors and corruption, what damage the brute force of emergency law-making did, and how we can avoid making the same mistakes again.

1. States of Emergency

A state of emergency changes everything, and everyone.

It can be triggered by any number of events, the most common being war, weather, famine and plague – classic threats to the existence of human societies. The emergency may last only for a few days, for example a catastrophic flood, or for years, as did the world wars of the twentieth century. But the measures in response tend to be similar, with the aim being to direct all of society's efforts towards addressing the threat. However, it is not easy to redirect the attention and efforts of millions of people towards a singular cause. They may not yet understand how the emergency will affect them and their family. Maybe they disagree with the government, or are unwilling to make personal sacrifices for the collective good. People want to get on with their lives. So there will often be some form of compulsion involved, through law and ultimately by force. The state can begin to appear authoritarian – that is, a state which is more focused on obedience than on personal freedoms.

Six features

The 'Emergency State' is my term for what happens when a state reorganises itself to tackle an existential threat. Like the emergencies which trigger them, Emergency States vary significantly. An Emergency State which develops when a society is fighting a war will focus on conscription of new troops and the manufacture of weapons. If a society is experiencing famine, the main purpose of the state will become to distribute scarce food and protect existing stock. But while there are differences, Emergency States tend to share six characteristics.

First, the Emergency State is *mighty*. When a state focuses its vast resources and attention on a single point it wields tremendous might. In that sense, the Emergency State is a kind of weapon, held in a glass-fronted cabinet with a sign saying *in case of existential emergency break glass*. In war, perhaps the most common trigger for the Emergency State, this is seen in the use of military power, swelled by vast sums of public money, the conscription of civilians into the armed forces, the requisitioning of publicly owned resources to build armaments, and the repurposing of scientists and engineers to accelerate technological innovation. The power and brute strength of the Emergency State can be the difference between a society surviving or perishing when faced with an existential threat. In the COVID-19 pandemic we saw a similar show of power, for example in the vast state effort involved in enforcing and paying for the lockdowns, the eye-watering resources spent on the test and trace system, and the rapid development and deployment of the COVID-19 vaccination.

But mighty power comes at a cost. In the Emergency State, open and democratic decision-making is replaced with a centralised and often opaque system. This is the second feature: *power is concentrated*.

Power in a democracy should be thinly and widely spread. We sometimes talk about a balance of powers – between the legislature (in the UK, the Parliament), executive (the government) and the judiciary (the courts). This has evolved over centuries. In the UK, Parliament is 'sovereign', which means, in theory at least, that it is the ultimate source of power – because it can pass laws, which must be followed by everyone. Those who make the law are also bound by it – that is what we call the rule of law. The government, consisting of the Prime Minister and his or her ministers, is usually formed by the political party which has the most seats in the House of Commons following a general election. It runs the country on a day-to-day basis, setting policy, drafting laws and deciding the direction of the country. Those elected to the House of Commons are responsible for upholding the interests of the people in their constituency. Ultimately, the 1,400 or so Parliamentarians, also including unelected members of the House of Lords, are responsible for passing those laws and holding the government to account.

In the ordinary course of things this thin spread of power is an advantage. It insures against knee-jerk decision-making which societies can come to regret later. Big decisions are taken slowly and deliberatively, allowing for different viewpoints to be heard. Debates take place not just in the Parliament chamber but in private and public spaces; a national conversation. Individuals may be caught in the crossfire of fierce words, but the state ultimately benefits. Adam Gopnik, the *New Yorker* writer and author, emphasises how important *conversation* is to the liberal state. Liberalism, he says, is 'based on reason and an appeal to argument, aware of human fallibility and open to the lessons of experience'.[1]

Liberal democracies also benefit from the scrutiny of courts, usually after a law comes 'into force' and its real-world impacts begin to be felt by individuals. It is useful to think of a developed liberal democracy as an efficient communications system, both designed and evolved to ensure that as much data as possible can be transmitted to decision-makers. This allows decisions to be made on as close to complete information as possible, allowing for the fact that in a large, complex society of millions of people there will never be *perfect* information, but at least there will be many inputs. This information can be obtained through various democratic channels, collated and inputted into the final decision, which will certainly a *better* decision than if the minister made it on the basis of their instincts, what they have read in the newspapers or (worst of all) what they take to be the mood on Twitter.

Emergencies put all of that out of balance. When the enemy is at the gate – or at least when it feels that way – decisions must be made quickly and authoritatively. This can turn the basic rules of democracy on their head. The deliberative delay which is usually a strength can suddenly appear a weakness, fiddling while the state burns. Decisions which ordinarily would require the highest level of consideration and due process must be made with unseemly speed. Similarly, the finite resources of the state will often have to be reallocated. One pot, such as funding for cancer care, may have to be raided to fill another, such as building an army fit for imminent war, or implementing a system to test and trace victims of a new virus. Power will inevitably become more concentrated as emergency authority is granted, usually to an individual or a small group who can act swiftly and ruthlessly. That authority will need to be supported by the use of physical force so that people can be compelled to act in a way which will lessen the threat. Parliament and the courts may have to be sidelined, or their roles diminished, because checks and balances are suddenly seen as dithering and delay. One consequence is that injustices proliferate, whether through disproportionate policies or heavy-handed policing. Events move so quickly, and the usual information flows become so disrupted, that thousands of injustices remain hidden. Even in a democracy, the state begins to take on characteristics of authoritarianism, such as centralised power, the bypassing of democratic institutions, the reliance on the police and security forces to enforce harsh laws and a general sense that society should be bent towards a single goal, with all other concerns becoming secondary and even superfluous.

Government by decree is radically different to the liberal democratic norm. At some point during the rush of coronavirus regulations which controlled our daily lives for two years, I realised that the regulations reminded me of the military orders which were the basis of the legal system during the British administration of south-eastern Iraq in the early 2000s. Earlier in my career I had needed to read through hundreds of pages of those orders as part of a war crimes inquiry. These rough and ready orders seemed so different to the tidy statutes which formed our law. But the regulations which were the legal basis of lockdowns and gathering restrictions were closer to military orders than ordinary laws.

The third feature is that Emergency States are *ignorant*. Decision-makers have to rely on limited and potentially unreliable information. The usual scrutiny from the legislature and courts is replaced by a random assortment of people who happen to have access to the leadership, such as financial backers or those with personal relationships, and who may have reasons not to bring bad news, for example if they owe their position to the leader's patronage or are afraid that they may suffer adverse consequences. Access to the leader becomes a priceless commodity.

Another cost of heavily concentrated power is *corruption*. This is the fourth feature of the Emergency State. If dissent is suppressed or even banned, there is nobody to tell leaders not to steal from the state or to create laws that benefit themselves and their own group. My experience of acting in cases involving institutional failings, such as disastrous hospitals or war crimes committed by the armed forces, is that although people tend not to see themselves as doing the wrong thing, most get swallowed up in the culture of the institution. It takes a very strong personality indeed to rise up against a dominant culture, and those who do speak out tend to be met with ridicule or other forms of victimisation. So it is no surprise that corruption spreads easily in a state which is sealed shut.

The fifth feature of the Emergency State is that it is *self-reinforcing*. C. K. Allen, a scholar of the emergency laws put in place during the Second World War, observed that 'the public had been frequently assured that they were merely "lending their liberty" . . . there were many promises and pledges of "freeing the people" . . . The whole history of the subsequent years shows . . . that government by decree, once made, is extremely difficult to unmake and that "emergency", once it has taken hold, is a very tough plant to uproot.'[2] Untrammelled power is addictive. Once a government becomes used to ruling by decree, the temptation will sometimes be to keep the powers which allowed them to do so for, as Allen suggested, a 'rainy day'. I will show in the final chapter that this is a real risk in relation to pandemic powers. The United Kingdom is, after all, a rainy country.

It is tempting, during the quiet times, to be sceptical about whether societies would succumb to the negative effects of the Emergency State. Surely we wouldn't allow our rights to be taken away, power to be concentrated, Parliament to be sidelined? But this is a mistaken assumption. The final feature of the Emergency State is that, often, we *want it to happen*.

Human psychology and emotion play an important role in how societies change during an emergency. You can *feel* an emergency. If you have ever experienced acute physical danger, it is possible to feel a similar sensation from observing, even if remotely, a threat to the nation. I can think back to a few such moments in my own life, such as when I watched the Twin Towers burning after the 9/11 terrorist attacks, or when I heard that the Prime Minister had been taken into intensive care after contracting COVID-19. Everyone will experience these moments differently, but there is a common experience of emergencies, likely arising from human evolution, which although grounded in fear and even panic can appear to *simplify* everything, lending us a sense of community and shared purpose. That shared purpose can be used for good – banging pots and pans to show support for the National Health Service – but can easily turn to bad: the scapegoating of the Jews in the 1930s by Hitler for the economic and social crisis that Germany was experiencing shows how emergencies, and the feeling of allegiance to an 'in' group, can be used to encourage discrimination against a minority group.

Another emotional aspect of emergencies is that we yearn for a strong leader to direct us out of whatever crisis we are facing. Leaders tend to become more popular during national emergencies, although the effect can be short-lived.[3] People also rally around the flag. Jonathan Haidt, a social psychologist, reports research that shows strangers will spontaneously organise themselves into leaders and followers when natural disasters strike. Haidt writes that when people see that their group needs to get something done they are happy to follow, as long as the leader does not 'activate their hypersensitive oppression detectors'.[4] He emphasises that humans do not, in fact, tend to follow blindly – and will react strongly against feelings of oppression – but that 'groupish psychology', pursuing a common goal in a community of trust, can be harnessed to achieve almost anything, good and bad.

One of the reasons I decided to become a human rights lawyer was the feeling I had, and that I observed in others, in the days and weeks after the 9/11 attacks. I had never really felt patriotic before, and yet there I was, briefly, feeling a surge of support for my country as it faced the new threat of international terrorism. I saw first-hand how a state of emergency could rearrange what previously appeared to be immutable foundation stones of a society, practically overnight. On 10 September 2001, terrorism was one of many concerns. After 11 September, it was *everything*.

It dominated the news, popular culture, our thoughts. I remember it as a kind of hysteria, where fear and panic drove away doubt and caution. Among other dangerous effects this had was a rise of Islamophobia and the scapegoating of Muslims, wrongly blamed for the actions of extremists.[5] Out of that heady mixture swiftly emerged stronger anti-terrorism laws which significantly curtailed liberties in the United Kingdom, leading to unlimited detention without trial, mass surveillance and house arrest for terrorist suspects.[6] It felt like living in a different country. As a child in the Jewish community I had learned about the horrors of the Holocaust, when an entire society conspired to murder millions of Jews. I had always assumed that this was a terrifying but unique historical event, which must have involved a society so different to my own that it might as well have happened on a different planet. But after 9/11, perhaps coinciding with entering adulthood, I realised that I had been naive.

Any human society can rearrange itself towards a cause, either good or bad. All it takes is a threat, followed by a series of lines being crossed as freedoms are gradually whittled away, and what would once have seemed extraordinary becomes quite ordinary – we *want it to happen*, even if we might regret our decisions once the heat of the emergency has subsided. As George Orwell wrote in 1945, just after the end of the Second World War, a time when our freedoms were 'lent':

> [T]he relative freedom which we enjoy depends on public opinion. The law is no protection. Governments make laws, but whether they are carried out, and how the police behave, depends on the general temper in the country. If large numbers of people are interested in freedom of speech, there will be freedom of speech, even if the law forbids it; if public opinion is sluggish, inconvenient minorities will be persecuted, even if laws exist to protect them.[7]

The rise of the Emergency State

A state of emergency can rearrange societies and generate public emotions of anger and fear, as well as of community and shared purpose – feelings which can be channelled to support a strong leader, to do both good and bad. The Emergency State is a mighty weapon. But tremendous power becomes concentrated, wielded by a strong leader and a small coterie of advisers, who are supported by the police and security services to take drastic action and even compel people to act in ways they otherwise would not. That swift and ruthless decision-making comes, however, at a cost. Concentrated power with little scrutiny can lead to ignorant decision-making and corruption. It results in many hidden injustices which may never come to light, or at least not until much later. It is a stress test for the liberal institutions such as Parliamentary democracy and human rights laws: sometimes those liberal institutions fail the test, illiberal measures emerge by diktat, power is wielded without accountability. And the vast powers can well outlast the emergency which was used to justify them.

This is what happened in the UK during the COVID-19 pandemic.

2. Very Strong Measures

31 December 2019 to 4 March 2020
Cases: 247
Deaths[1]: 3

On 31 December 2019, officials informed the China office of the World Health Organization (WHO) that they had detected cases of pneumonia in Wuhan City, Hubei Province of China, with an unknown cause. On 12 January 2020, China shared the genetic sequencing of severe acute respiratory syndrome coronavirus 2 (SARS-CoV-2), the cause of coronavirus disease (COVID-19). The WHO was told that the outbreak was associated with exposure in a seafood market in Wuhan City. By 20 January, cases had been reported in Thailand, Japan and the Republic of Korea. Three people in Wuhan City had died after contracting the virus.[2]

On 27 January 2020, with the death toll at eighty, the Chinese government imposed a 'lockdown', a stay-at-home order, in Wuhan and other cities in Hubei Province. This affected 57 million people. Transport in and out of the cities was prohibited, all shops were closed except those selling food or medicine, private vehicles were banned without special permission, and travel outside the home was limited, with some areas restricting outings to one family member every two days. Enforcement was strict, with officials visiting homes to enforce isolation for anyone found with COVID-19 symptoms – though this did not prevent up to five million people fleeing Wuhan in anticipation of lockdown measures, many of them travelling to crowded megacities such as Beijing or Shanghai, or flying out of the country, potentially seeding further outbreaks.[3] All non-essential businesses in Shanghai were shut and schools suspended.[4] The country's top body, the Standing Committee of the Chinese Communist Party, headed by President Xi Jinping, took direct control of operations. Meanwhile, cases of COVID-19 had been reported in at least thirteen other countries, including France, Australia, Canada and the United States.

The WHO declares an emergency

A declaration of an emergency is always a trigger moment. The most important example in the early days of the pandemic happened on 30 January 2020. The Director-General of the WHO has the power, under the International Health Regulations (IHR) 2005,[5] to declare a 'Public Health Emergency of International Concern' if there is an unusual and unexpected event with a serious impact on public health and a significant risk of international spread and international travel or trade restrictions.[6] We will hear more about these regulations later, in relation to the origins of our own lockdown laws. For now, it is important to understand that states which sign up to the IHR have a duty to report public health emergencies, and once a Public Health Emergency of International Concern is formally declared, they have legal obligations to respond promptly and comply with WHO recommendations.

On 30 January, the WHO declared the novel coronavirus outbreak in China to be a Public Health Emergency of International Concern. It also issued a warning to the rest of the world that they should be prepared for containment, including active surveillance, early detection, isolation and case management, contact tracing and prevention of onward spread of the coronavirus, and must 'place particular emphasis on reducing human infection, prevention of secondary transmission and international spread'.

The WHO commended the 'very strong measures' that China had taken to contain the outbreak – by that date tens of millions of citizens were locked down – which the WHO said were 'good not only for that country but also for the rest of the world'.[7] The steer to the rest of the world was clear; they would soon face the new virus, and it was 'still possible to interrupt virus spread, provided that countries put in place strong measures to detect disease early, isolate and treat cases, trace contacts, and promote social distancing measures commensurate with the risk'. Although the declaration made no mention of the word 'lockdown', any world leader watching the footage of what strong measures looked like in China, and reading the declaration, would have seen lockdown as a, if not *the*, way to control the spread of the novel coronavirus. A few days earlier, Pope Francis had praised China's 'great commitment' to containing the outbreak.[8]

Responding to the WHO's declaration, the UK's four Chief Medical Officers advised that the national threat level be raised from low to moderate, and that the UK governments 'escalate planning and preparation in case of a more widespread outbreak'.[9] They said that it was likely there would be individual cases. That was proved correct when the first confirmed COVID-19 cases were announced the following day, 31 January, at the Royal Victoria Infirmary in Newcastle – two Chinese nationals who had been staying in York. Press reports confirmed that eighty-three Britons evacuated from Wuhan to RAF Brize Norton in Oxfordshire had been quarantined at Arrowe Park Hospital in Wirral.[10]

Events were now moving very quickly. On 10 February, the UK Scientific Pandemic Influenza Modelling Committee reported that outbreaks outside China could not be contained by isolation and contract tracing. If a high proportion of asymptomatic cases were infectious, they said, then these policies would not contain the spread. They estimated that the number of confirmed cases in China was at least ten times higher than the official number, and that there was a realistic probability that there was already sustained transmission in the UK which would 'become established in the coming weeks'.[11]

On the same day, there was a significant event in the context of our story. The first coronavirus law appeared: The Health Protection (Coronavirus) Regulations 2020.[12] These regulations shared many of the concerning features of the emergency law-making which, unknown to anyone at the time, would continue for over two years.

How laws are made

To understand the first set of coronavirus regulations, and what would follow, we first need to know about two different kinds of laws, and *why* they are different.

Primary legislation is an act of Parliament, sometimes also called a statute. Acts start as bills introduced in either the House of Commons or the House of Lords. They tend to go through multiple stages in each House before being approved by both. Crucially, this will include days or even weeks of scrutiny, debate, amendment, consideration by committees – and even something wonderfully called 'ping pong', when amendments go 'to and fro' between the Houses. The final stage, after approval by both Houses, is royal assent by the Queen – thankfully, in our constitutional monarchy, a formality. After that, the bill becomes an act – for example, my favourite law, the Human Rights Act 1998 – and is the law of the land, unless and until it is amended or repealed.

The other kind of law is secondary legislation, also known as delegated or subordinated legislation, which is subordinate to an act of Parliament. An act of Parliament will sometimes give a power – usually to government ministers – to make secondary legislation, usually in the form of something called a statutory instrument. The justification for this kind of law is that the modern state is complicated and that to regulate such a complex environment we need *a lot* of laws. Parliament can only scrutinise so much, so while the big, important laws are subjected to the gold standard act of Parliament procedures, with all of the debates, amendments and ping pong, the finer detail is left to statutory instruments. As the UK Parliament's website puts it, statutory instruments fill in the details of acts and provide practical measures that enable the law to be enforced and operate in daily life.[13] The convenient thing about statutory instruments, from a minister's point of view, is that if they need to be approved by Parliament at all,[14] they will only need a 'yes or no' vote, generally by both Houses – there is no prospect of Parliament making amendments, that is, editing the text to make it better. And they are almost always approved: the last successful motion to stop a statutory instrument was in 2000 in the House of Lords, and 1979 in the House of Commons.[15]

You could think about statutory instruments as children who always need an act of Parliament as a parent. And the parent of The Health Protection (Coronavirus) Regulations 2020, the first coronavirus law, was an act of Parliament called the Public Health (Control of Disease) Act 1984, which from now on I will refer to as the Public Health Act.[16]

Where emergency powers come from

It may have seemed that the emergency laws which responded to the emerging pandemic came out of nowhere. In the eye of the storm it can seem that everything is new and unprecedented, but often the truth is that similar things have happened before. The danger of forgetting is failing to learn lessons, and repeating mistakes. This book is about the emergency measures put in place to attempt to contain the coronavirus, and the impact those had on individuals and the state. Before I investigate that, it is important to set the context. Emergency powers have a *long* history.

Many states, including the UK, have emergency enabling laws on the statute book which, if a state of emergency is declared, trigger strong powers usually for use by the government. Those powers will typically allow the government to enact laws to do whatever is needed to contain the emergency, sometimes bypassing the legislature for expediency. This idea goes back a long way. Ancient Rome had a formal procedure for emergencies called *justitium*. When the Republic faced existential threats, the highest magistrates or senators would appoint a 'dictator' with sweeping powers, and suspend the role of the law courts.[17] The earliest recorded occasion of *justitium* being invoked was in 465 BC, when the Romans believed they were about to be invaded by the Aequi, a belief that turned out to have been mistaken. Virtually all civil affairs and operations could be suspended by decree.[18] The Senate retained financial control, and appointed dictators were subject to term limits of six months. *Justitium* extended to the power to shut public businesses, including those businesses with the potential to hinder the *justitium*.[19] The cessation of the *justitium* would be pronounced by a decree of the Senate or the same magistrate that enacted it. The power to appoint dictators was used ninety-five times over 300 years, until a dictator, Julius Caesar, decided not to give the emergency powers back.[20]

In the modern world, the vast majority of constitutions contain a mechanism to declare states of emergency and enable fundamental constitutional rights to be temporarily disapplied. In the human rights context, emergency measures must be 'strictly required' and time-limited, and the rights to life and to have 'no punishment without law', and the prohibition of torture and of slavery, cannot be disapplied – 'derogated from' – even in a time of emergency. Ten European states derogated from some of the rights contained in the European Convention on Human Rights towards the beginning of the COVID-19 pandemic, for example in order to ban public assemblies which would ordinarily be protected by the right to freedom of assembly.[21]

Lending our liberty during the Second World War

The UK government has rarely relied on such extreme measures. It was eighty years ago, during the Second World War, when the country was last ruled by government decree:

> [T]here was scarcely a department of public or private life which was not under governmental control . . . Huge codes of detailed sub-laws, frequently amended, had grown . . . Against this measure of grievous emergency there was no effective appeal and very little means of objection, while the provisions for compensation were obscure and complex . . . there were some 1,700 prosecutions every month for offences against the Regulations . . .[22]

This account of the wartime regulations by C. K. Allen bears striking similarities to what we have just experienced, and is a valuable insight into common themes during states of emergency.

The laws created to help Britain win the war against Hitler were extensive and extraordinary. 'Private property had yielded on a vast scale', Allen says, 'to national necessity'. Under the Defence Regulations, the War Office requisitioned 700,000 acres of land for military purposes. Even six years after the war, the Ministry of Supply still held over 3,000 buildings. In 1948, there were 95,000 houses requisitioned to provide accommodation to the homeless. There was concern that a flurry of criminal offences were being created by statutory instrument – as many as 700 by the end of the war. Tens of thousands of people were prosecuted each year of the war, even though it was sometimes 'transparent that the accused persons did not know and could not have known of the passage of the particular instrument under which he was to be convicted'. One troubling example cited in Parliament was the leader of a small religious order who was prosecuted for buying eggs. He had bought them at more than the controlled price from a small supplier, described as a 'widow entirely dependent on her small trade'. Neither knew the controlled price had been changed by a recent Order. The magistrates expressed 'disgust and astonishment' that the matter hadn't been dealt with by advice and a caution, but were compelled to convict and give out a fine.[23]

The war legislation, and similar powers which remained in force many years after the war ended, 'virtually gave *carte blanche* to executive discretion', Allen says. The Attorney-General of the time, Sir Hartley Shawcross,[24] admitted that the purpose of the legislation granting emergency powers was to circumvent any legal challenge – clearly not just a gripe of modern politicians. Indeed, the Defence Regulations resulted in one of the most infamous of all English legal cases, *Liversidge v Anderson*,[25] a 1941 judgment of the House of Lords, then the most senior appeal court in the UK. Sir John Anderson, the Home Secretary, had detained Robert Liversidge, a businessman, using emergency powers which allowed him to detain a person indefinitely if he had 'reasonable cause to believe' they were of 'hostile origin or associations' or had recently been concerned in various acts 'prejudicial to the public safety or the defence of the realm'. Four of the judges decided that the Home Secretary did not need to say *why* he had made the decision, but merely to confirm that he had the required 'reasonable cause to believe'. In other words, it was enough for him to say 'trust me'.

Reading the judgment, it is clear that the majority of judges were deeply concerned that the matter was one of national security. Rather than interpret 'reasonable cause to believe' as it normally would have been, giving the courts the responsibility of reviewing the underlying rationale of the decision, Lord Macmillan said it was 'right so to interpret emergency legislation as to promote rather than to defeat its efficacy'. In other words, emergency laws are *different*. Lord Atkin, a single voice among the law lords, vociferously disagreed. He accused the others of being 'more executive-minded than the executive'. He went on to say, in a dissent which would echo through the ages:

> In this country, amid the clash of arms, the laws are not silent. They may be changed, but they speak the same language in war as in peace. It has always been one of the pillars of freedom, one of the principles of liberty for which on recent authority we are now fighting, that the judges are no respecters of persons and stand between the subject and any attempted encroachments on his liberty by the executive, alert to see that any coercive action is justified in law.

Lord Atkin's dissenting judgment is what law students now learn. But the majority decision is just as important, as it demonstrates a truth about how judges (and others) can behave during a national emergency, straining themselves to defer to the executive, terrified that by acting independently they will disrupt the national emergency response. By doing so, Lord Atkin went on, they contort themselves like a character in Lewis Carroll's *Through the Looking-Glass*. Perhaps we could say that Lord Atkin's approach is how we would like to imagine ourselves behaving during such a crisis, but the four-judge majority better indicates how we *tend to* behave when faced with the brute force of emergency power. We *want it to happen*.

In Allen's view, writing in 1965, the post-war emergency powers probably represented the 'high-water mark of governmental powers in the whole history of English legislation'. Indeed, at the time of writing almost two decades later, he remarked that certain elements of the Defence Regulations remained in place: '[t]hese ogres are not yet dead', he said, but are suffering 'death by the thousand cuts'. He relates the grimly amusing history of the post-war emergency powers, as the Conservative and Labour parties took turns to criticise each other for retaining the same excessive powers. Freedom, says Allen, 'is not easily gained, and, once surrendered – however necessary the surrender may be – is even less easily regained'. This is because there is always the argument, as made by the government in a 1953 Parliamentary debate, that 'we would perhaps be well advised to keep a particular power for a rainy day'.[26] Allen tells us, back in 1965, that in the post-war debates there was a growing uneasiness about the 'lack of effective Parliamentary check on delegated legislation'. The more things change, the more they stay the same.

The vast powers given to the government during the Second World War and beyond differed in some respects to the COVID-19 powers we saw in 2020 to 2022. But in many ways they were similar, granting government the power to micromanage the lives of everyone living in the UK, all the way down to whom we socialised with and when we could leave home, a power which applied twenty-four-hours a day and for months at a time. The regulations were ever-changing, at times deeply confusing and almost impossible to challenge. The comparison between the two periods was obvious to those who knew their history, such as Lord Justice Hickinbottom, ruling in late 2020 on one of the most significant legal challenges to coronavirus regulations, who said they were 'possibly the most restrictive regime on the public life of persons and businesses ever – certainly, outside times of war'.[27]

As I have said, no state of emergency is the same, but the states that emerge share many similar features, the defining one being that we, the public, are asked to, and often willingly do, lend our liberty to the cause of fighting an existential threat. Why do we do it? And how can we ensure our liberty is safely returned?

The stroke of the minister's pen

The vast and at times illiberal Defence Regulations of the Second World War were made under the Emergency Powers (Defence) Act 1939. What would be the 2020 equivalent as the COVID-19 pandemic arrived at our shores?

We now need to talk about the Public Health Act.

The date on the act is 1984, a fact that some lockdown sceptics used to brand the law Orwellian. But in substance this is a much older piece of legislation, going back to the first version in 1848. It was designed to lay the foundations of 'sanitary reform',[28] the key aims of which were addressing health inequalities and preventing the spread of infectious diseases such as cholera.

You will not find the power to impose lockdowns in the 1984 version of the Public Health Act. Instead, its powers to control communicable disease included barring infected persons from places of work or education, and detaining someone in hospital if they were infectious.[29] These powers could be exercised by a minister making regulations – in other words, subordinate legislation.

These limited powers were occasionally used by ministers. One famous example is depicted in Russell T Davies' *It's a Sin*, a

2021 television series about the beginning of the UK AIDS crisis in the 1980s. In a harrowing scene, one of the young protagonists, suffering from HIV, finds himself in an empty hospital ward. When he tries to leave the room, he is blocked by a police officer. His mother is told that her son cannot leave because he is 'infectious' and the authorities have been 'granted a court order for his detention under the Public Health Act of 1984'. When she asks whether there is anything to stop her taking him out of here 'right now', the official replies, frostily, 'the law of the land forbids you'. The scene is frightening not just because of the visceral depiction of the then little-known disease, but also the feeling that the shadowy bureaucracy of the state was assaulting the family as much as the illness itself.

The incident was based on a true story.[30] In 1985, a 29-year-old man with AIDS was reported to be the first person confined in a hospital under a 'new anti-AIDS law', a statutory instrument made under the Public Health Act.[31] After what was described as a five-minute hearing, a magistrates' court ordered his continued detention at Monsall Hospital in Manchester.[32] Following major protests and a second court hearing, the man was allowed to leave hospital after ten days, when it was considered he no longer needed to be detained.[33] That 1985 statutory instrument, passed by then Health Secretary Ken Clarke, was severe – it allowed a person to be detained in a hospital without being heard at court. Those who are familiar with mental health laws in this country may not be surprised by the powers available to public authorities when a person's detention could be justified by the 'protection of the public'. But as oppressive as these laws can be, the powers are focused on individuals, not groups.

In early 2020, Matt Hancock, the Minister for Health and Social Care, will have been briefed by his officials on what powers were available to him to control the spread of the novel coronavirus, rapidly appearing over the horizon, speeding in from multiple locations. But he will have been told about a very different Public Health Act to the one which Ken Clarke used to try to prevent the spread of HIV. Because, since 1984, the Public Health Act has been extensively amended, and the minister's powers under it *turbocharged*.

The impact of SARS

To understand how, and why, the Public Health Act 1984 became the *enabler* of the Emergency State, we need to take a detour via Geneva, and the headquarters of the World Health Organization.

The United Kingdom is a founding member of the WHO and signed its constitution in 1946.[34] Article 21 of the WHO constitution grants the World Health Assembly the power to adopt regulations about 'sanitary and quarantine requirements and other procedures designed to prevent the international spread of disease'. In 2005, at the 58th World Health Assembly, the regulations were updated. Why? Because the world had just experienced the Severe Acute Respiratory Syndrome (SARS) outbreak. SARS, like COVID-19, is a coronavirus which was first identified in China. It appeared in November 2002, the WHO was notified in February 2003, and the outbreak was finally contained by 2004.[35] It infected 8,096 people and caused at least 774 deaths worldwide.[36]

The 2005 changes to the International Health Regulations were intended to fix the problems exposed by the outbreaks of SARS and another dangerous disease, Ebola. One such problem was the dependence on notification by countries of new outbreaks. China had been criticised for the four months it took to notify the WHO of the first SARS cases, which likely led to the outbreak taking longer to contain.[37] And so, when the International Health Regulations came up for review, tighter notification requirements were put in place. The Public Health Emergency of International Concern process was introduced to co-ordinate global co-operation during an international health crisis. The key message was that states were required within five years to strengthen their public health response capacities so they could rapidly respond to new public health emergencies, and implement any recommendations for public health measures made by the WHO.[38] The WHO was saying to states that they needed to be ready: the next health emergency might not be as containable as SARS. The WHO was vague, however, on the kind of measures states might use – the purpose of the regulations was to control the 'international spread of disease in ways that are commensurate with and restricted to public health risks, and which avoid unnecessary interference with international traffic and trade'.[39] The focus was on quarantining and isolating travellers to prevent the spread of an infectious disease from country to country. The regulations were also clear that all such measures should be 'with full respect for the dignity, human rights and fundamental freedoms of persons'.[40] Notably, the IHR did not explicitly authorise – or mention – large-scale lockdowns, which was no surprise given that by 2005 there hadn't been any.

Within three years, the UK Parliament did as the WHO required. In 2008, the Public Health Act was amended explicitly to implement the International Health Regulations 2005.[41]

A suite of new powers was added to the Public Health Act, giving ministers the ability to do practically anything 'for the purpose of preventing, protecting against, controlling or providing a public health response to the incidence or spread of infection or contamination in England', including restrictions on gatherings, travel, children attending school and almost unlimited requirements 'on or in relation to persons, things or premises'. And if the minister declared that 'by reason of urgency, it is necessary to make the order without a draft being so laid and approved' by Parliament, it would be possible for there to be no Parliamentary scrutiny or approval for twenty-eight days after the law had come into force – or, if Parliament was in recess, even longer.

When the changes were debated in Parliament, only a few saw the breadth of the implications. On 21 May 2008, the seventh day of debate in the House of Lords,[42] one member[43] was eerily prescient when he said:

> [I]t is a very sweeping power indeed. I say that because we are dealing here with measures which are not defined in the Bill but which Ministers can bring into force more or less at the stroke of a pen without the prior approval of a magistrate . . . Ministers, by regulation, are being given considerable power to limit and constrain the daily lives and freedoms of citizens.

He asked for an illustration of the kinds of provisions which regulations were likely to contain in the event of 'say, a SARS outbreak', and why there was apparently such a low threshold for requirements to be placed on persons, things and premises. Another member[44] raised concerns that the new powers for ministers did not have the same safeguards as those under the Civil Contingencies Act. A government minister responded, giving three examples of the kind of measures the government had in mind: recalling a contaminated cargo which had been dispersed across the country; requiring all individuals working with poultry to wear protective clothing and undertake a decontamination regime to prevent the spread of avian flu; and empowering hospitals to require all visitors to SARS patients to wear protective clothing to reduce the risk of onward spread. In the very brief debate in the House of Commons, one MP said it was 'curious' that the measures in this bill received 'almost no attention' despite being 'quite draconian'.[45]

Social distancing is old but national lockdowns are new

Quarantine and movement restrictions were discussed in the 2008 debate, but what we would now call lockdowns were not. Baroness Finlay, a cross-bench member of the Lords and medical doctor, said she was 'full of admiration' that during the SARS outbreak the 'Hong Kong community managed to clamp down on its movements, including self-quarantine on the part of healthcare workers'. There needed to be powers to 'impose cautious behaviour', she claimed, 'because I fear that in this country we may not do as well as Hong Kong'. The 2002–4 SARS outbreak had led to city-wide restrictions including school closures, compulsory quarantine for infected persons and, in Hong Kong, a guarded quarantine of a housing estate, under laws which had apparently not been invoked since an outbreak of bubonic plague in 1894.[46] Perhaps Baroness Finlay was unaware that legal compulsion, as well as voluntary compliance, was used in Hong Kong.

As the three examples given by the government minister show, by May 2008 the idea of a national, or even city-wide, twenty-four-hour lockdown was not one in the world's contemplation, let alone that of the UK Parliament. The quarantine of a housing estate during the SARS outbreak is a huge conceptual distance from the kind of national lockdowns which became commonplace by spring 2020.

The first truly national 'lockdown' in the modern age, by which I mean stay-at-home orders applying to everyone except essential workers, appears to have been in Mexico in May 2009, during the swine flu outbreak, imposed for five days on 111 million people after ninety-nine confirmed cases and eight deaths from the virus.[47] 'There is no safer place than your own home to avoid being infected with the flu virus,' Felipe Calderón, Mexico's President, told the nation on 29 April 2009.

National lockdowns may be a new development but emergency responses to pandemics have involved similar features for centuries. It has been recognised for hundreds of years that people gathering together cause certain kinds of disease to spread, meaning that public authorities have often used guidance, and laws backed up by the threat of law enforcement and even physical force, to prevent people mixing and disease spreading. This has included travel restrictions, quarantine of the potentially infectious, isolation of the sick, curfews (a kind of lockdown), social distancing measures, gathering bans and compulsory face coverings. The World Health Organization praised Mexico for giving the world a model of 'aggressive control measures'.[48]

Plagues were well known to the ancient world, and emergency powers were used to attempt to control them. The Plague of Justinian of AD 541–549, thought to have caused up to 10,000 deaths per day,[49] led to a dictator-like figure being appointed on a limited term – an early example of a formal Emergency State.

Many of the tactics societies still use today to control the spread of infectious diseases were developed in the Middle Ages. The word 'quarantine' has its origins in the Black Death (bubonic plague) pandemic of the 1300s, which may have caused as many as 200 million deaths. Bubonic plague is an infection which is now known to spread by fleas, often carried by rats on ships, and which causes high fever, pain, headaches and large swollen lumps in the lymph nodes (buboes) which develop and leak pus. The idea of quarantine is to separate and restrict the movement of people after they have been exposed to a contagious disease, to see if they become ill. This is different to isolation, which is separation and restriction of movement of people who *are* ill, though the words are often used interchangeably. The first known quarantine law was passed by the Venetians in 1377, mandating quarantine for thirty days. This later evolved into forty days because forty was seen as a holy number,[50] reflecting

Lent and biblical stories such as Moses spending forty days receiving the Ten Commandments and Noah being at sea for forty days during the Flood – the number is reflected in the word itself, from the French *quarante*.

England has used emergency laws to contain plagues for over four centuries. 'Plague Orders' were first enacted in England in 1578 following a bubonic plague outbreak, and then reimposed during further significant outbreaks. Measures such as the order to shut up infected houses for forty days were widely declared by 1550.[51] The orders varied widely by region. In 1540, a Liverpool bye-law forced the infected to live in cabins on the heath in the summer and stay at home with their windows and doors closed during winter. In 1550, watchmen stationed on the Ouse Bridge in York ensured that the infected did not move across the city. In Exeter in 1564, infected people were banned from the streets.[52] The Aldermen of the City of London were reticent to act and only started forcing infected Londoners to isolate, and hired watchers and searchers to monitor compliance, in 1563.

National laws soon followed, and it is remarkable how similar they were to the social distancing laws passed over 400 years later during the COVID-19 pandemic. The laws were 'specially directed and commanded' by Queen Elizabeth I because her unruly subjects who 'by very disorder, and for lacke of direction do in many partes wilfully procure the increase of this general contagion'.[53] In 1578, Plague Orders were put up throughout England, in churches, marketplaces and other locations where people congregated. For the many who could not read, they were read out. There were seventeen rules, including punishments for quarantine-breakers, a 'plague tax', the burning of the clothes and bedding of the dead, and the suppression of 'dangerous opinions'.[54] Local magistrates were required to produce reports on the number of deaths and cases overall in each parish which were in turn centrally reported and collated.

Londoners who lived through the COVID-19 lockdowns would have recognised much of what Daniel Defoe wrote about in his *A Journal of the Plague Year*, recounting his experiences of the 1665 bubonic plague outbreak.[55] There were bans on social gatherings, including 'all plays, bear-baitings, games, singing of ballads, buckler-play, or such-like causes of assemblies of people', with any rule-breaker 'severely punished by every alderman in his ward'. All public feasting was banned, together with an impressive policy that the money spared 'be preserved and employed for the benefit and relief of the poor visited with the infection'. Ale-houses and taverns could still open, but 'disorderly tippling' (drinking) was banned and all venues were to be shut by nine each evening. Begging was also prohibited and disobedience punished. Similar restrictions appeared around the world. In 1683 in Marseille, it became a legal requirement for any person thought to have plague to be quarantined and disinfected. Also during the 1680s, ports in North America introduced quarantine to prevent the spread of yellow fever.[56]

In the centuries that followed, similar plague control measures were seen regularly. During cholera outbreaks in the nineteenth and twentieth centuries, societies emulated strategies developed in response to bubonic plague. This led to the use of 'lazarettos', quarantine ports, in France. At other European ports, ships were barred entry if they had 'unclean licenses', that is, were arriving from regions with known cases of cholera.[57] Any traveller who had come into contact with the infected or had travelled from an area where cholera was known to be spreading were quarantined. Those who were known to be infected were forced to isolate in lazarettos. In 1836, in Naples, health officials restricted the movement of, and arrested, sex workers and beggars, who were considered carriers of cholera.[58] In Sardinia, armed men patrolled the coast to stop anyone disembarking from ships. It was the only Italian region which appears not to have suffered a cholera outbreak.

The 1918–20 influenza pandemic, also known as Spanish flu, infected around 500 million people worldwide and is estimated to have killed at least 50 million.[59] While public health infrastructure and authorities were significantly better prepared to deal with the influenza pandemic than they had been for the bubonic plague, systems for alerting public health authorities did not generally include influenza, meaning the response to the disease was delayed. Several island nations quarantined themselves pre-emptively, including Iceland, Australia and American Samoa. Australia required ships arriving from infected countries to quarantine for seven days. Public health officials at the state level agreed to notify the Commonwealth government of any detected cases of the flu, to control traffic in and out of the state and to require residents to obtain a permit before moving internally within Australia.[60] Across the world, social distancing measures were introduced, including closing schools, theatres and places of worship,[61] though there was significant variation between and within countries as to how the outbreak was tackled.

In the UK, the focus was on minimising contact with others, although, there being no national health service at the time, the response was decentralised and sporadic and never extended to national rules.[62] Cheltenham Boys' School locked staff and pupils inside the building to protect them from exposure. In Sunderland, election candidates decided not to canvas door to door, while across the country social venues such as churches, theatres, cinemas and dance halls were shut for long periods.[63] In the United States, face coverings became a common sight, and in some places compulsory, but even then there was significant resistance from parts of the population. The Anti-Mask League of San Francisco was established in response to a local mask ordinance, with up to 5,000 supporters at one point.[64] A 2007 study of the response of forty-three cities across the US to the

1918 influenza pandemic found there was a strong association between early and sustained 'nonpharmaceutical' interventions, for example school closures, public-gathering bans, isolation and quarantine, and significantly reduced excess deaths.[65]

The rise of lockdowns

The SARS outbreak of 2002–4, however, gave a preview of the kind of harsh national measures which we would see with COVID-19. Despite or maybe because of huge publicity, only 8,096 cases and 774 deaths worldwide were recorded and the virus was contained in a way which its sequel, COVID-19, also known as SARS-CoV-2, could not be.

The first case of SARS was traced to Foshan, China, and to workers in the food and hospitality sectors in particular.[66] The Chinese government initially refused to share intelligence with public health bodies and discouraged reporting. Singapore's response was stark. In March 2003, it began to enforce compulsory quarantine of any infected person and announced that all primary and secondary schools and junior colleges were to be shut. On 30 March, Hong Kong authorities quarantined Block E of the Amoy Gardens housing estate due to a 200-case outbreak in the building. The balcony was completely closed and guarded by the police. The residents were later transferred to the quarantined Lei Yue Mun Holiday Camp and the Lady MacLehose Holiday Village because the building was deemed a health hazard – strong measures later praised in the UK Parliament and used to justify the emergency law which would underpin the COVID-19 lockdown.

In 2014–16, an Ebola outbreak affected Sierra Leone, Guinea and Liberia, and infected close to 30,000 people, killing over 11,000, with half of all cases occurring in Sierra Leone. Ebola can lead to haemorrhaging, bleeding and bruising among other symptoms, and often death. In September 2014, the Sierra Leone government declared a state of emergency and imposed a three-day lockdown on its population.[67] Community workers and volunteers were employed to provide door-to-door surveillance and public health information. After the lockdown ended, quarantine restrictions were put in place in high-risk areas, with the curfews imposed lasting for weeks or months. Schools were closed in May 2014 and only reopened in April 2015 as the epidemic began to slow. Most students lost around thirty-nine weeks of schooling as a result.[68] Significant travel restrictions were enacted, not just in countries where cases were detected but also in those limiting arrivals from affected countries.[69]

COVID-19 spreads, as do lockdowns

Now we can return to that first set of UK coronavirus regulations, which appeared on 10 February 2020 and looked a lot like the 1985 regulations that allowed for the detention of the young man with AIDS at Monsall Hospital. The regulations permitted people to be screened if exhibiting coronavirus symptoms, or generally when arriving in the UK, and potentially detained if they were suffering from the 'Wuhan novel coronavirus'. Importantly, the regulations also gave the Secretary of State the power to make a 'serious and imminent threat declaration' when the 'incidence or transmission of Coronavirus is at such a point that the measures outlined in the regulations may reasonably be considered as an effective means of preventing the further, significant transmission of Coronavirus'. The Secretary of State could now declare an emergency and trigger emergency powers.

But on 10 February 2020 the Secretary of State had not yet pulled the trigger. That happened four days later, when Matt Hancock made a 'serious and imminent threat' declaration, so triggering the first set of emergency coronavirus powers.[70] At that stage there was no suggestion from the government that a lockdown was imminent. Within a few weeks, that would change, and the state of emergency which had been declared on Valentine's Day 2020 would last until 18 March 2022 – for over two years.

On 23 February, Italy imposed lockdown measures in several northern cities, including ordering residents to stay at home and avoid social contact, and closing schools and non-essential shops.[71] But, as in China, the threat of a local lockdown may have made things worse, with up to 30,000 students boarding trains to their families in the south of Italy – and many of them being forced into quarantine when they arrived. In their excellent book on the history of quarantine, Geoff Manaugh and Nicola Twilley point out that the situation in Italy demonstrates that 'when faced with an imminent quarantine order, large portions of a targeted population are almost guaranteed to flee, sometimes carrying the disease with them'.[72] On 3 March, Australia used the obscure Biosecurity Act 2015 to authorise restrictions on the movements of people suspected of having coronavirus. The law had previously been used to stem outbreaks of disease among livestock.[73]

Lockdowns were spreading as quickly as the virus itself.

3. Take It on the Chin

5 March 2020 to 23 March 2020
Cases: 12,320
Deaths: 935
Cumulative deaths: 938

It is easy to forget, now that we have become used to the idea of lockdowns, how radically strange those first few weeks of the pandemic were.

On 4 March, I recorded an episode of my podcast with the *New Yorker* writer Adam Gopnik. By the time we sat down to record, something which would become impossible in person within three weeks, the idea of city- and even state-wide lockdowns had travelled from faraway authoritarian China almost to the UK's eastern shores. Both Gopnik and I had seen the startling videos emerging from Northern Italy, where part of the country had been cut off and locked down, and hospitals were buckling. It was rapidly becoming clear that coronavirus would be a major event for every society to grapple with, and almost impossibly difficult decisions would have to be made. Whom to treat, when medical capacity runs out? Which freedoms to remove, to protect life and health?

I said at the time that observing each country's reaction was like putting a sort of radioactive dye through different countries' political systems. There had been news that Iran had a far larger outbreak than was officially being reported, and illicit mobile phone videos showing the digging of mass graves. Gopnik suggested that authoritarian societies have difficulties dealing with dynamic threats, but that China, on the other hand, 'seems to have dealt with it well by using extreme authoritarian measures', perhaps because it was a *well-organised* authoritarian society. But he also questioned whether a virus with a 1 per cent mortality rate should lead us to shut down freedom of movement, circulation and conversation simply in order to eliminate that risk. We agreed that moments of panic and fear were dangerous times for democracies and Gopnik said it was at these times that we 'look for the big daddy who will reassure us and make us safe'. We had a gentle disagreement about whether Jack Bauer from *24* or Bruce Willis's character in the *Die Hard* films was the archetypal rule-breaking, niceties-smashing guy whom societies crave in danger times. As it turned out, it was a third fictional character: the mayor in the film *Jaws*, who keeps the beach open despite the clear evidence of a giant shark stalking the ocean and to whom Boris Johnson repeatedly compared himself.[1]

The UK's first COVID-19 death

On 5 March, a UK hospital reported the first death following COVID-19 infection, a woman in her seventies who died at Royal Berkshire NHS Trust.[2] By that day, the number of people diagnosed with the virus had reached 116, a rise of more than thirty in twenty-four hours. The Prime Minister's spokesperson told the BBC that it was 'highly likely the virus is going to spread in a significant way', although on the same day Boris Johnson told ITV's *This Morning* that there was a theory that the UK 'could take it on the chin, take it all in one go and allow the disease to move through the population without really taking as many draconian measures'.[3] It is now clear that this was a viewpoint he sympathised with.

On 8 March, Italy placed more than 16 million people under quarantine in Lombardy and fourteen other central and northern provinces, together with closing schools, gyms, museums, nightclubs and other venues across the country. The BBC reported the measures to be the 'most radical taken outside China'. These were extended to a countrywide quarantine on 9 March.[4] The next day, I tweeted that the idea of 'effectively putting everyone under house arrest' would lead to 'mind-boggling' legal issues. 'What would they do', I asked, if someone broke the rules? 'What lawful force could they use? [It] would have to be proportionate to the threat posed by millions of non-infectious people.'

Little did I know.

On 11 March, the WHO declared COVID-19 a pandemic, another trigger moment. It also announced that there had been 118,000 cases in 114 countries and 4,291 deaths; compare this with the total death toll of SARS over two years of 774. The WHO Director-General warned of 'alarming levels of spread and severity' and also 'alarming levels of inaction'. If there had ever been any doubt that the WHO was urging countries to implement lockdown measures, it was put to rest by a statement which argued that several countries had 'demonstrated that this virus can be suppressed and controlled' and praised measures being taken in Iran, Italy and the Republic of Korea, albeit acknowledging that the measures were 'taking a heavy toll on societies and economies, just as they did in China'. The WHO did emphasise that 'countries must strike a fine balance between protecting health, minimizing economic and social disruption, and respecting human rights', but how they were to achieve that in the oncoming social carnage was anyone's guess.

The delay phase

The following day, 12 March, the UK government abandoned its 'contain' phase, which focused on contact tracing people who had travelled into the country from coronavirus hotspots, and entered what officials called the 'delay' phase. For the first time, anyone who showed coronavirus symptoms was asked to stay at home, regardless of whether they had travelled to affected areas.[5] The Prime Minister, in an address to the nation, called coronavirus the worst public health crisis for a generation. 'I must level with you . . . with the British public,' he said, looking uncharacteristically grave, 'many more families are going to lose loved ones before their time.'

I remember watching the announcement, and feeling a jolt at those words. It was already obvious that this was not going to be another swine flu or SARS, crises which had generated fear and some panic but had seemed to fizzle out. But the message from the Prime Minister, at that stage, was about deploying lines of defence 'at the right time to maximise their effect', and only relatively mild measures were announced, such as advising vulnerable people not to go on cruises, recommending that people with symptoms isolate and everyone wash their hands. Schools would not be closed because 'this could do more harm than good at this time'. Sir Patrick Vallance, the government's Chief Scientific Adviser, said that the aim was to reduce and broaden the peak and 'build up some degree of herd immunity', a comment that led to fierce debate over the government's apparently lax approach to the virus, symbolised by the 50,000 fans allowed to watch Liverpool play Atlético Madrid at Anfield on 11 March while the rest of Europe was banning large gatherings. It appeared that the UK government was not looking to emulate what some were calling 'Continental-style' lockdowns. At a meeting of the Scientific Advisory Group for Emergencies (SAGE) the following day, the group was unanimous that 'measures seeking to completely supress spread of Covid-19 will cause a second peak' and concluded there was a 'near certainty' this would occur in countries such as China where 'heavy suppression' was underway.[6]

A human rights response?

As the threat level grew and lockdown measures were looking far more likely than I had imagined, I started to think seriously about what a human-rights-respecting response to the deadly new virus would be. On 15 March, I began a Twitter thread on human rights and coronavirus.[7] My aim was to share thoughts and resources as the crisis unfolded, and more generally to try to frame the inevitable debates over restrictions from a human rights perspective. At that point, I did not expect to be posting the 228th tweet in the thread over a year later. I strongly believed that human rights were essential for framing the hard decisions we would inevitably need to make as societies attempted to contain the virus. This was, after all, what human rights were intended for – as a checklist of freedoms, a blueprint for a free society, and as a sophisticated concept of proportionality, which were designed to balance rights such as family life and free expression against social imperatives such as public health. But the signs were not good: to date this had not been a government given to prioritising human rights.

What do I mean when I talk about rights? In a constitutional democracy, such as the United States, Germany or France – and many other countries – the constitution sits above everything else. It will describe the basic rights of the people who live under the power of the state. Those rights are interpreted and enforced by the judiciary – usually a supreme or constitutional court, which will be the ultimate decider of what the constitution means, and whether a law conforms with it or not. In the UK, we do not have a formal constitution which can be found in a single document, but we do have an array of rights and duties contained in various legal instruments. Some are quite ancient, such as the right in the 1215 Magna Carta not to be imprisoned, dispossessed, outlawed, exiled or 'ruined in any way' without the lawful judgment of our peers and the law of the land, or the rights in the 1689 Bill of Rights not to be taxed without Parliament's agreement, to free speech in Parliament and not to be subjected to 'cruel and unusual punishments' (that is, not to be tortured). Other rights are quite modern, such as those contained in the European Convention on Human Rights (ECHR), an international treaty of 1950 which was developed after the Second World War. When the ECHR was drafted, the world had just experienced a truly existential crisis: two world wars in quick succession, genocide and the 1918 influenza pandemic.

The ECHR was strongly supported by Britain, particularly Winston Churchill, the wartime prime minister, and David Maxwell Fyfe, a Tory politician who had prosecuted Nazi leaders at the Nuremberg war crimes trials. In 1946, Churchill described the 'tragedy of Europe', a continent reduced to 'a vast, quivering mass of tormented, hungry, careworn and bewildered human beings, who wait in the ruins of their cities and homes and scan the dark horizons for the approach of some new form of tyranny or terror'.[8] He proposed a movement for European unity, at the centre of which 'stands the idea of a Charter of Human Rights, guarded by freedom and sustained by law'. The aim of this charter was to preserve what was seen as the essential core of liberal societies against the dark and ever-present threat of authoritarianism.[9]

Relaxed, sceptical and unarmed

A democracy does not *fall* suddenly into authoritarianism, but it can *slide*. It is therefore useful, when considering the dangers of flirting with authoritarianism, even if it is for the laudable aim of fighting an existential threat, to consider the lessons of Europe's twentieth-century authoritarian experiment and how the modern human rights movement emerged from it.

In 1949, Pierre-Henri Teitgen, a French Resistance fighter and a founder of the ECHR, remarked that European citizens had thought personal freedom was like 'the air they breathed – with the result that they did not perhaps esteem it highly enough', so when fascism, Nazism and communism descended, 'they found us relaxed, sceptical and unarmed'. The Second World War made Europeans 'realise afresh the value of humanism', that is, societies founded on reason, science and compassion.[10] But how? The solution reached by these battle-weary freedom fighters was a simple list of rights and responsibilities, protected by law. Drawing on the 1948 Universal Declaration of Human Rights, the rights in the ECHR were mostly civil and political, such as freedom of expression, religion, privacy and family life, and the right to a fair trial, to marry, to not be discriminated against, tortured, enslaved or detained without lawful authority. The first right on the list was the right to life.[11] The ECHR was certainly drafted with pandemics in mind, demonstrated by the inclusion in Article 5, the right to liberty, of an exception for 'the lawful detention of persons for the prevention of the spreading of infectious diseases'. It is no surprise that the drafters saw the need to allow for quarantine; infectious diseases were a major threat during the first half of the twentieth century.

The power of the ECHR is that every state which signed it is obliged, in international law, to 'secure' the rights and freedoms contained within it and to 'abide by' the decisions of its court.[12] The European Court of Human Rights is based in Strasbourg and officiated by an equal number of judges from each signatory state.

Fundamentally, the ECHR is a check on the actions of states which would guard against tyranny. It sets out not just the basic rights of individuals but a blueprint for a liberal society where people of all races, faiths, nationalities, genders and other personal characteristics could live in peace and flourish; freedoms tragically out of reach in the first half of the twentieth century, when democratic institutions had been overwhelmed by the brute force of totalitarianism. And, as Teitgen astutely observed, it would be a mistake to assume that totalitarianism begins with the complete capture of a society. Rather, 'evil progresses cunningly . . . one by one freedoms are suppressed' while 'public opinion and the entire national conscience are asphyxiated'.[13]

The metaphor of asphyxiation is apt in this story, but it also points to an important truth often forgotten in times of peace and prosperity: authoritarians do not always take power by force – sometimes they are invited. Hitler was a popular figure in Germany in the 1930s, offering downcast Germans a means to restore national greatness, pride and prosperity through 'racial purity'.[14] With this in mind, a key aim of the ECHR was to install an early warning system. Any society where the basic rights set out in the ECHR were being whittled away, even if gradually, was one which was *vulnerable* to tyranny. The ECHR would be a doctor standing vigil beside her patient, Europe, constantly watching for the tell-tale signs of disease which, if not treated, might ultimately be fatal. And as lockdowns were imposed across Europe, and rights more severely limited than at any time since the Second World War, that early warning system would be given its most important test since it came into force in 1953.

A vast and rather odd law

By 17 March 2020, France, Spain and the Netherlands had joined Italy in imposing their own lockdowns. The French President announced that the country was 'at war', with the army helping move patients to hospitals and police enforcement of the new regulations.[15] On the same day, the WHO in Europe called for the 'boldest actions' to fight coronavirus and warned that 'even draconian measures may not stop, but [only] slow down' the spread of the virus. The fear of the spreading virus, and rapidly climbing case and death rates, appeared to overwhelm any hesitation caused by the relative novelty of national lockdowns.

In the UK, 17 March was a landmark day for coronavirus laws when the first and, to that date, only piece of coronavirus primary legislation appeared in draft form. Unlike the months of debates, votes and amendments usually required to pass primary legislation, the Coronavirus Bill took eight days. It was debated for around six hours in the House of Commons and seven and a half hours in the House of Lords, and given royal assent on 25 March. The bill's 329 pages and over 135,000 words would, among other things, water down the legal duty to meet the care needs of eligible people, grant police stronger powers to quarantine infected people, give the government more powers to ban gatherings, change the rules for inquests (investigations into deaths) to make it easier to hold a coronavirus death investigation without a jury, postpone upcoming local and mayoral elections for a year, weaken safeguards for detaining people under mental health law, give the Scottish government equivalent powers to those that the Westminster government had under the Public Health Act, and relax judicial safeguards on the power of the Home Secretary to order the interception of communications.[16]

This was a vast piece of legislation which demanded full scrutiny and debate, not a perfunctory few hours. And it is no surprise in those circumstances that only very limited amendments were made by Parliament, the most significant being that instead of the act automatically being in place for two years, it would have to be reauthorised every six months by Parliament.

But even this apparent concession to scrutiny was not quite what it seemed; Parliamentarians could only vote 'yes' or 'no' when reauthorising and could not propose amendments. This would be a sham process, making a mockery of Parliamentary scrutiny, because the Coronavirus Act was bound to be reauthorised – no MP would want to be held responsible for scuppering the entire act for a single concern. The Coronavirus Act could therefore be *approved but never improved*. This pattern would be repeated on countless occasions with the coronavirus regulations. In the cases of both the Coronavirus Act and the coronavirus regulations, had the government used the Civil Contingencies Act 2004, which did allow for amendments and had far stricter requirements for Parliamentary involvement, it would have led to substantive participation by the legislature, rather than the symbolic but essentially meaningless votes which were held over the next two years, when Parliament would begin to resemble a nodding dog.

So why did our government pass new primary legislation, the Coronavirus Act, in such a short time, instead of using the already existing Civil Contingencies Act 2004 (CCA)? The CCA gives ministers very significant powers to make new regulations and could have been used to do nearly all of the things the Coronavirus Act ultimately did.[17] However, it also contained strong democratic safeguards, such as Parliament having to approve any emergency regulations within seven days of them being 'laid', giving Parliament the opportunity to amend regulations, and regulations lapsing thirty days after they were made. And why not use the CCA to pass the myriad coronavirus regulations which would follow? The government said in 2022 that it decided not to use the CCA because the Public Health Act was already available and the CCA should only be used as a 'last resort'.[18] Dominic Cummings, the Prime Minister's Chief Adviser at the time, however, said that the CCA was disregarded because the government was advised by the Cabinet Office that if it relied on the CCA the courts would strike down regulations, 'causing chaos', and that is why emergency primary legislation was used. There was, he said, 'no time for proper analysis'.[19] The selection of the solution which would give the government most power, and which was the least open to challenge, was deliberate.

You might be wondering how the government produced a 329-page bill, containing an array of complex new laws, in just a few weeks. I always suspected they took most of it off a dusty shelf marked 'emergency pandemic powers', and it turned out I was right. The Coronavirus Bill was based on the Pandemic Flu Bill, a bill developed in secret sometime between 2016 and 2020 by Westminster and the devolved administrations, whose existence was not made public at any stage before the Coronavirus Act came into force and which received no scrutiny from the public or Parliamentarians. We can only speculate as to why this fact was only revealed by the government to a Parliamentary committee in 2022, but I agree with that committee that developing the bill in secret took away the opportunity for meaningful scrutiny.[20]

The Coronavirus Bill was also interesting for what it was missing. It did not contain powers to impose restrictions on people's movements in England. It did contain such powers for Scotland and Northern Ireland,[21] because the Public Health Act did not apply to those parts of the UK, so they needed to be given equivalent powers. It would have been hugely beneficial for democratic accountability and scrutiny if the government had asked Parliament to debate and approve powers to lock down the population – and not rely on the wide and vague powers in the Public Health Act, which, as we saw, were approved by a Parliament that had no warning as to how they would eventually be used.

There was no lockdown plan

Why was there no opportunity in the Coronavirus Bill for Parliament to authorise lockdowns? One simple fact, once known, makes sense of those two weeks leading up to the lockdown announcement on 23 March: even as late as 18 March, five days before the Prime Minister's 'you must stay at home' edict, the government was not planning a lockdown. Dominic Cummings has revealed that there was no lockdown plan by 18 March, and that SAGE had not included a potential lockdown in its modelling for that reason.[22] On 19 March, the Prime Minister's spokesperson declared there was 'zero prospect of any restriction being placed on travelling in or out of London'. He also dismissed claims that people could be fined if they left their homes – both policies which would be announced four days later.[23] The 'slow and gradualist' approach to non-pharmaceutical interventions (that is, restrictions on movement and gathering) was, according to a Parliamentary report,

> not inadvertent, nor did it reflect bureaucratic delay or disagreement between Ministers and their advisers. It was a deliberate policy – proposed by official scientific advisers and adopted by the Governments of all of the nations of the United Kingdom.[24]

One reason for the reticence was that the government was advised by SPI-B, the behavioural group of SAGE, that the British public would not accept a lockdown or an East Asian-style track and trace system and the infringements of liberty it would cause.[25]

My focus here is not the effectiveness of the early approach (though it now appears to have been too slow), but the impact it had on law-making. Because of the last-minute nature of the decision to impose a lockdown, the government was in a sense bounced into law-making. Rather than using the precious weeks in February and March to strategise, and consult, on the best way to make coronavirus laws, it seemed to be flailing wildly, legislating on the hoof and grabbing for what it saw as the least troublesome method. The 23 March decision to lock down appears to have been so rushed that the law to enforce it on the population was not ready for another three days, a rush which also explains the curious absence of any power to lock down the population in the Coronavirus Bill which was speeding through Parliament that very week. The Science and Health Committees say that during those early weeks of March there appears to have been:

> a policy approach of fatalism about the prospects for covid in the community: seeking to manage, but not suppress, infection. This amounted in practice to accepting that herd immunity by infection was the inevitable outcome, given that the United Kingdom had no firm prospect of a vaccine, limited testing capacity and there was a widespread view that the public would not accept a lockdown for a significant period.[26]

Dominic Cummings informed the committees that on 14 March he and Helen MacNamara, Deputy Cabinet Secretary (who, three months later, would bring a karaoke machine to an illegal lockdown party),[27] told the Prime Minister 'you are going to have to lock down, but there is no lockdown plan. It doesn't exist. SAGE hasn't modelled it.' They were going to have to 'hack together' a plan. The government's own modelling was now showing that if more severe measures were not taken – and quickly – hundreds of thousands would die and the National Health Service would be overwhelmed.[28] Then, on 16 March, SAGE considered a paper from Imperial College London which predicted 510,000 deaths in an 'unmitigated' epidemic, following which SAGE recommended 'additional social distancing measures' to be introduced within days. This proved to be a key factor in persuading the government to instigate a full lockdown.[29] On the same day, the Prime Minister used his national televised address to advise the entire UK population, not just those with symptoms, to stop all non-essential contact with others and all unnecessary travel. It looked as though, he told the nation, we were 'now approaching the fast growth part of the upward curve'. Without 'drastic action', the Prime Minster warned, 'cases could double every five or six days'.[30] On Thursday 18 March, he announced that schools were to close from Friday afternoon, to apply 'further downward pressure on that upward curve', and warned that the government would 'not hesitate to go further, and faster, in the days and weeks ahead'.[31]

More than just arguing in Parliament

However quickly events were moving, with decisions being made at speed, based on rapidly evolving science, it is clear that Parliamentary scrutiny and accountability were low on the government's list of priorities. As Cummings has said, the government's priority in the first emergency phase was the fear that COVID-19 could kill hundreds of thousands of people, not 'arguing in Parliament'. And at that stage in the pandemic, you might be thinking: *fair enough*. This was a genuine emergency, and a week in which the Prime Minister was told that if the UK continued its current trajectory half a million people could die. It is difficult to imagine a more obvious time when the Emergency State would be a necessary evil, involving power being handed to an individual or small group for a short period and usual democratic processes being curtailed or even suspended. But, as will become clear, something else was going on too, beyond what was required by the emergency – something far more dangerous for democracy.

A significant risk of the Emergency State is that you cannot choose the leader who happens to be in charge when the emergency happens. If you are lucky, he or she will have the qualities needed not just to manage the crisis in hand but also to ensure that democratic institutions can be returned to more or less their pre-crisis state. Boris Johnson may or may not have had the skills to manage the public health response to the COVID-19 pandemic, but in March 2020, he and his team had no real regard for Parliament or democratic accountability. Johnson had only been in power for two months when the Supreme Court ruled that his government unlawfully attempted to shut down, or 'prorogue', Parliament for five weeks in order to ensure the UK left the European Union. It is worth recalling the words of Lady Hale and Lord Reed, then President and Deputy President of the UK Supreme Court, in that judgment – words which should have guided the government's response to the pandemic, but instead were studiously ignored:

> Let us remind ourselves of the foundations of our constitution. We live in a representative democracy. The House of Commons exists because the people have elected its members. The Government is not directly elected by the people (unlike the position in some other democracies). The Government exists because it has the confidence of the House of Commons. It has no democratic legitimacy other than that. This means that it is accountable to the House of Commons – and indeed to the House of Lords – for its actions, remembering always that the actual task of governing is for the executive and not for Parliament or the courts.[32]

Rather than show any remorse over the unprecedented constitutional chaos it had caused, Johnson's government would use the prorogation judgment as a pretext for reducing the powers of the courts to hold government to account, through attempts to weaken judicial review and replace the Human Rights Act with the first bill of rights in a democracy which would actually reduce rights protections. It is therefore no surprise that when the pandemic hit, 'arguing in Parliament' was seen by the government as a hindrance, to be dispensed with as swiftly as possible. The problem is that while many leaders may have done the same thing in the first days, few would have made sidelining Parliament a feature – and certainly not a bug – of the Emergency State which would persist for two more years. Over these next two years, of the 109 regulations that imposed restrictions, only nine would be voted on by Parliament before they came into force, and forty-two were never debated at all. With the government imposing the most severe restrictions on freedom for eighty years, this was nothing short of a democratic tragedy.

4. You Must Stay at Home

24 March 2020 to 1 April 2020
Cases: 30,354
Deaths: 4,264
Cumulative deaths: 5,202

> As Matt Hancock, the Health Secretary, had put it to Boris Johnson, slamming his hand on the table: 'We've got to tell people that they can't do anything unless it is explicitly allowed by law.' Legally, that was a revolution even if it was meant to be time-limited. Normally, people are free to do what they like unless the law prohibits it. But Matt Hancock's radical suggestion, which he described as Napoleonic, flipped that British tradition. In lockdown, people would be forbidden from doing anything unless the legislation said, in terms, that they could.
>
> Matthew d'Ancona, Tortoise Media, 19 June 2020[1]

On the first day of lockdown, I cycled from my home in Finchley 'to work'. Not to go to my workplace in Doughty Street, as we had been told to work from home. Indeed, the Coronavirus Act would have a huge impact on my working life because it permitted, for the first time, online court hearings. So the small study in my house quickly became a workplace and courtroom, the place where we hung the washing – pushed just out of camera view – and, as I was regularly invited to explain the new laws to the public, a TV studio too. The kitchen table had become a schoolroom for my children. But, for those strange first days, I kept up my routine of cycling to work, then turning immediately back. I suppose that I wanted to hold on to some semblance of routine, though I wondered if I was like one of those Japanese soldiers who kept fighting after the Second World War ended.

I was also grimly fascinated to see the new reality. Central London had become a ghost town, with shops and restaurants closed and streets practically deserted. I am sure that many will remember that those first few weeks were also incongruously sunny.[2] I hurtled down Archway Road, thinking what a treat it was to cycle down a road usually full of traffic, in the beautiful sunshine, when I saw two figures emerging from an ambulance wearing full hazmat suits. Suddenly the scene was transformed to something more sinister.

I wondered what it reminded me of. Perhaps a post-apocalyptic zombie film, as many were suggesting? No, because in those images the streets tend to bear the scars of the apocalypse itself, with shops looted and widespread destruction of property. The streets of London looked pristine, but shuttered and empty. I realised the image evoked a Stephen King novella I had read as a teenager called *The Langoliers*. The story begins with a plane flying through a strange light in the sky. Upon landing at an airport, the passengers find that it is completely deserted, with no power. They discover they have entered a time rift where they are trapped a few moments behind normal time, rendering the world dull and lifeless, beautiful but threatening. That was the feeling I had – that the world had unexpectedly paused.

Where was the law?

Meanwhile, trying to make sense of this strange new reality, I and other lawyers were left guessing as to what the Prime Minister had meant when he said, on Monday 23 March, that if people don't follow the rules, the police 'will have the powers to enforce them'.[3] What powers? From where? And when would they arrive? On that bright Tuesday, and indeed on Wednesday too, no such powers existed. Meanwhile, I was already being criticised for raising this publicly – as it might discourage people from following 'the rules' – and so I tweeted that this wasn't about legal pedantry but about ensuring that the police were exercising powers which were clear and accessible, for them and for citizens.[4] I asked a question which I assumed the police were asking themselves too: what would they be doing on the beat today? Did they know whether the Prime Minister's statement was 'rules or advice', and would they be arresting people without lawful authority? Even at the time it seemed obvious that planning for this eventuality was strangely lacking, despite it being apparent for some weeks that restrictions were coming, and that there was a real risk that the 'bond of trust' between state and citizen would be broken if it turned out that what was being described as a 'rule' was in fact merely advice or imploring.[5] I would have been startled to know then how important the confusion between rules, guidance and law would become and, over the next two years, how threadbare the bond of trust between state and citizen would grow.

Jonathan Sumption, a former Justice of the UK Supreme Court, also sounded the alarm on the morning of Thursday 26 March, in a *Times* editorial.[6] He saw a link between the lockdown 'rules' (at that stage still only guidance) and the 'growing power of the state', which was, he said, as with laws relating to terrorism and climate change, not driven by power-grabbing politicians but by 'popular demand'. The price of public pressure for action would be the 'destruction of personal liberty, livelihoods and sociability'. The Prime Minister in his press conference had 'placed most citizens under virtual house arrest', but under our constitution even strong advice does not have 'the slightest legal effect without statutory authority'. Sumption warned of the dangers of legislation in general language which 'can be used for purposes far removed from the original intention' and that governments armed with vast powers are usually reluctant to part with them, citing the example of wartime regulations which were not repealed until 1964.

It is interesting to read Lord Sumption's 26 March article now, in light of him later being seen as the intellectual voice of the anti-lockdown movement. I often disagreed with him, essentially because I was always wary of people – particularly if they had no scientific expertise – who confidentially asserted that lockdowns were unjustified. Looking back now, it is clear that Lord Sumption had already decided that lockdowns could not work and were unlikely ever to be justified. I did sometimes envy those who were so sure in their opinions on the appropriate interventions to suppress a virus we still knew little about, except that it was spreading like wildfire and already killing thousands. I always accepted that he and other lockdown sceptics might ultimately be proved right, but despite the obviously severe impact lockdowns would have on some of our rights, I could not in good faith join in their opposition when there were so many in the scientific community who said that lockdowns were, to paraphrase Churchill on democracy, the worst intervention except for all the other forms which had been tried.[7]

Napoleon returns

The emergency regulations which would enforce the lockdown finally appeared on Thursday 26 March, at around 3 p.m., three days after the Prime Minister had instructed the country to stay at home. The law had come into force two hours before it had been published, and an hour and a half before it was shown to

Parliament. My understanding from those who know is that work did not begin on the regulations until the day of the Prime Minister's announcement, which is why they took almost three days to appear. Compared to what would come later, they were simple, almost simplistic. Just eleven pages, a tiny creature compared to the bloated monsters which would emerge later in the year.

The Health Protection (Coronavirus, Restrictions) (England) Regulations 2020 were made under the power given to the Health Secretary by the Public Health Act. They did three things: banned people from being outside the place they were living without a reasonable excuse, prohibited gatherings of more than two people in public places and forced non-essential businesses to close. The use of the term 'lockdown' can be confusing, as for many people this included later restrictions on gatherings. I should say now that the way I am using the word 'lockdown' in this book is the same way the government uses it: a 'stay-at-home' order, expressed in law as the prohibition against leaving home without a reasonable excuse.

It is difficult to emphasise how extreme, oppressive and quite frankly *strange* this law was. If the quote at the beginning of this chapter attributed to Matt Hancock is accurate, he was right to say that it flipped the usual maxim of English law – that everything which is not forbidden is allowed – on its head.[8] When the law came into force, it instantly and severely restricted the basic rights of everyone in England – in many cases, not just restricting but *prohibiting* the most basic activities of life: socialising, working, worshipping, sitting on a park bench, taking exercise, even hugging – important elements of what makes us human. When, in 2008, the changes to the Public Health Act were being debated, Earl Howe had worried that sweeping measures which were not defined in the bill could be brought into force at the stroke of a minister's pen. That is exactly what happened.

At 1 p.m., at the exact moment Matt Hancock signed the new

law, it came into force, and instantly and radically altered the relationship between citizens and the state. If Hancock did describe the rules as 'Napoleonic', he was probably referring to the Napoleonic Code, which the French leader established in 1804 to rationalise French law, replacing a hodgepodge of feudal laws with a single code. But the emphasis of the French Civil Code, as it is now known, is to make the law clear and accessible to the average person. There is a lot to be said for the idea of a civil code – particularly when you compare it to UK law, which is a jumble of statutory and common law that is essentially inaccessible unless you have, or can buy, legal expertise. I detect an element of British exceptionalism in his comment: assuming the French legal system in particular and 'Continental' legal systems in general are somewhat illiberal but could be borrowed temporarily for this emergency. Hancock might equally have called the laws 'draconian', as many did. But this expression has also become something of a misnomer. Draco, the first recorded legislator of ancient Athens, replaced the previous system of oral law with a written code which could be read by all literate citizens and enforced only by a court of law. Because the laws were so harsh, death being the punishment for almost every crime, his name has become a byword for oppressive laws. But, like Napoleon, he was also an innovator.[9] Ironically, the coronavirus regulations proved to be neither clear nor accessible and did as much to confuse and confound as they did to assist people in understanding what their severely restricted rights were.

There were two serious problems with the regulations. First, they became law without a debate, let alone a vote, in Parliament. The Public Health Act allowed ministers to bring in emergency regulations without Parliament's advance approval if 'by reason of urgency, it is necessary' to do so and, ordinarily, regulations would have to be approved within four weeks. But since Parliament was in recess, the clock started ticking only when it returned. The result was that the most severe restrictions on liberty in British history were not debated and approved until 4 May 2020, almost six weeks later.[10] When they were introduced to Parliament, the spokesperson for the opposition, Justin Madders, agreed the regulations were required but said that 'a couple of hours' debate – weeks after they were introduced – cannot in future be sufficient to provide the level of examination and scrutiny that such sweeping laws require'. Madders hoped that any new regulations would be debated in the House of Commons before being implemented. This was not to happen, nor would his plea that future rules be 'harmonised with advice, guidelines and all forms of official communication' be heeded.

And that was the second problem: the new law was at odds with the Prime Minister's announcement just three days earlier, on 23 March. He had declared that people could only leave their home for very limited purposes – he mentioned four, which were then published as guidance: shopping for basic necessities as infrequently as possible, one form of exercise per day, medical need or helping a vulnerable person, and travelling to and from work when this was 'absolutely necessary and cannot be done from home'. The law was materially different. Transport Minister Grant Shapps told BBC Radio 4's *Today* programme on 31 March 'people know the rules that have been set. Try and shop just once a week – just, you know, just do the essentials not everything else.' But there was no limit on shopping for basic necessities, no limit on the number of times people could exercise, and working outside the home did not have to be 'absolutely necessary'. The constantly sloppy language from ministers trying to explain the 'rules' was not just incompetence, it directly flowed from the inconsistencies between guidance and law.

Another source of confusion was that as soon as the lockdown began, the law in the four constituent parts of the United

Kingdom diverged. Throughout the pandemic, England, Wales, Scotland and Northern Ireland all had different rules because health was, it would appear, a devolved matter – that is, the power to manage it is contained in legislation which gives the devolved administrations certain powers to manage their own affairs.[11] I say 'it would appear', as I do not think this was inevitably the case: if the UK government had considered at the outset of the crisis that it wanted to direct the public health response in all four parts of the UK, it could have mandated this, for example through the Coronavirus Act. However, this may have increased political tension between the four nations at a time when there was already enough to worry about. The result was that enforced social distancing policies diverged across the four nations, sometimes in relatively minor ways and sometimes more significantly. In March 2020, the devolved administrations closely co-ordinated their responses and diverged only slightly. The leaders of the devolved administrations, Nicola Sturgeon (Scotland), Mark Drakeford (Wales) and Arlene Foster and Michelle O'Neill (Northern Ireland), participated in meetings of the Civil Contingencies Committee (COBR) chaired by the Prime Minister. However, by early June 2020 these committees were replaced and the leaders of the devolved nations no longer invited, so although there was still some co-operation it does not appear to have been at the same level. This perhaps explains why policy began to diverge more significantly from the summer of 2020. But none of this helped the public understand the increasingly complex rules.[12]

The very thin blue line

For many people, the criminal law had gone from being something which affected their lives only peripherally (such as paying taxes or following road safety laws) to being at the very centre. Everyday questions became legal conundrums. Is an Easter egg a basic necessity which could justify a trip to the shops? Should I rest on a park bench while exercising? Can I visit my 69-year-old parent to help them with basic tasks, even though only those aged seventy and over were defined as 'vulnerable'? *Can I leave the house?*[13] These were not theoretical questions, but real and urgent. And who was to determine the answers? One of the defining features of the Emergency State is that it hands enormous power to the police as enforcers of the regulations. I imagine that most police officers never expected to decide whether a person was committing a crime by buying an Easter egg. Policing is usually about enforcing public order; almost without warning, the police were now to focus on enforcing public health.

The regulations made it a criminal offence to do anything which contravened them, such as leaving the home without a reasonable excuse. Police were given extensive powers of enforcement: they could use reasonable force to remove people to their homes if they were outside without a valid excuse; they could use force to disperse gatherings; they were even given the extraordinarily wide power to 'take such action as is necessary to enforce any requirement'. After a rule breach had occurred, police could charge people with an offence, with no need to involve the Crown Prosecution Service (CPS), the experts in charging complex offences. But criminal prosecutions are long-winded and bureaucratic, involving rules of evidence, lawyers and courts. It would have been impossible for the police to prosecute thousands of crimes in the middle of a pandemic when it wasn't even clear the already backlogged courts would be open. So it made sense for police to be given the power to hand out 'Fixed Penalty Notices' (FPNs), essentially a 'ticket' which allowed people to avoid being prosecuted for an offence if they paid a fixed amount of money within a set time period. At the beginning of the first lockdown, FPNs were set at £60, or £30 if you paid within fourteen days of being notified. The penalty would then double for each subsequent FPN. The amount would later rise, for some offences astronomically.

Although it was regularly reported by the media that an FPN could be challenged in court, this was not actually the case. There was no process of appeal or review. Either you paid within twenty-eight days or, if the police thought it appropriate, you would be charged with the offence. The reality on the ground, however, was that if an individual's lawyer wrote to a police force pointing out an error in the FPN, the police would sometimes rescind it rather than face legal proceedings. For example, when I acted for students who were given £10,000 FPNs for allegedly organising house parties, we wrote to the police force pointing out that one student was out for the evening, returned to find a party and immediately went upstairs to bed. The police reversed their decision. But this was not a formal process and relied on individuals happening to have the resources and inclination to instruct lawyers. Ten thousand pounds is a life-changing amount of money for most people and practically impossible to pay, so it might be worth paying for lawyers to dispute the FPN. But for the vast majority of people who were given one, it would make no financial sense to instruct lawyers to challenge it. And police could give an FPN if they 'reasonably believed' that a person had committed an offence under the regulations. This granted them huge power, but also (to paraphrase Spider-Man's uncle, among others) great responsibility, to exercise their 'reasonable belief' fairly and – crucially – to familiarise themselves with the law they were tasked to enforce.

Some police failed to do so. One of the defining features of rule by coronavirus regulations was police overreach. During the first lockdown, police forces were variously mocked and castigated. On 30 March 2020, Cumbria Police tweeted 'Non-essential reasons for travel, Pitlochry to Wakefield via Cumbria to pick up a puppy. One of many stop checks this morning to check the necessity of travel.'[14] On 1 April, Glossop Police published guidance on Facebook saying that 'we have all been instructed to avoid all UNNECESSARY TRAVEL' and people are 'entitled to exercise once daily'. After public uproar the post was taken down. A number of police forces set up roadblocks so they could question motorists as to whether their journeys were essential.[15] Derbyshire Police used drones to track people exercising outside in the Peak District and even tweeted a video of drone footage featuring the caption 'WALKING YOUR DOG IN THE PEAK DISTRICT – NOT ESSENTIAL'.[16] They defended their actions by saying that the 'emergency laws were unclear'.[17] But there was no law restricting unnecessary travel or exercise – the confusion had clearly sprung from the Prime Minister's announcement and the government guidance, which was different to the law.

At the end of March, Neil Basu, Assistant Commissioner of the Metropolitan Police, pleaded in the *Daily Telegraph* that the public 'not judge too harshly' as not every police response will be 'sure-footed' and 'some will spark healthy debate'.[18] Within a week, the National Police Chiefs' Council (NPCC) produced useful guidance to make it easier for police forces to understand the new laws. 'We don't want the public sanctioned for travelling a reasonable distance to exercise,' the guidance said, and, in an obviously pointed reference to Derbyshire Police, 'checks on every vehicle is [*sic*] equally disproportionate'. NPCC, Police Federation and College of Policing were to issue, on the same day as the first lockdown law, the '4Es' guidance – Engage, Explain, Encourage and Enforce, with enforcement being the 'last resort'.[19] The emphasis was to move through the phases, meaning most police intervention would begin (in theory at least) with explaining the rules to people and trying to get them to comply voluntarily. Only if that failed would the police move through the gears towards FPNs and ultimately the use of reasonable force and prosecution.

Many people had a lockdown hobby. Some learned to knit or bake. Mine was stopping police on the beat on streets and in parks to ask what they thought the rules were. A week after the first lockdown began, I saw two Metropolitan Police officers patrolling a park. I stopped my bike (having been out for my lawful exercise) and asked what they were up to. They said they were focused on 'engaging and explaining', but if they needed to enforce they would. They referred to the 'four reasons'. I presumed these were from the Prime Minister's speech. I asked if they knew what was in the regulations. They said they did – but as became clear after a few more questions, plainly did not. As an example, they explained that if they saw me on my bike later that day they would stop me to have a word and maybe give me a fine. I told them there was no power in the regulations to give a fine for exercising twice in a day, and that this was only contained in non-legally binding guidance. They said it would have to be a 'test case'.[20] I repeated these questions a number of times over the months that followed and invariably found that the police, and council enforcement officers, had at best a shaky understanding of the law. As the rules became more complex, this just got worse. During the first lockdown, the police only had to worry about eleven pages of regulations. By the third lockdown, the law was over a hundred pages long, leaving the police in an even more difficult position, and the public exposed to enforcement of the wrong rules. After all, most enforcement relied not on courts applying the criminal standard of proof (having to be 'sure' an offence had been committed) but upon an individual officer's reasonable belief.

This was a recipe for many individual disasters. The '4Es' policy was important because it attempted to set the tone for policing, with police encouraged not to move directly to enforcement. But it would only work if officers had enough of an understanding of the law to explain it accurately, and enforce it appropriately. Why should a person go back to their home, or accept a police 'explanation', if they knew the police were getting the law wrong? What haunts me about the two years or so when 118,978 FPNs were issued,[21] and over 2,000 people prosecuted,[22] is that many thousands of people were wrongly handed a criminal penalty. How do I know this? Because the CPS reviewed prosecutions under both the coronavirus regulations and Coronavirus Act and found that, by August 2021, out of a total of 2,393 prosecutions, 740 were incorrectly charged. That is 30 per cent. Of the 295 prosecutions under the Coronavirus Act, every single one was incorrectly charged. And if you extrapolate the figure of 30 per cent wrongful charges to FPNs, that could mean as many as 40,000 were wrongly given. This will not just have been a £60 ticket – some FPNs were for thousands of pounds.

And it gets worse, because the CPS reviewed only 'finalised prosecutions' under the regulations – that is, where individuals pleaded not guilty. A large number of prosecutions were concluded using the 'Single Justice Procedure', a truly Kafkaesque process by which a magistrate and legal adviser read the details of the case and deliver a verdict, in private, without hearing from the individual charged. This process is usually used for much simpler offences, such as failures to pay for a TV or driving licence, but was extended to coronavirus regulations offences in June 2020.[23] It is obviously inappropriate for complex offences involving coronavirus regulations. And yet the procedure may have been used for close to 2,000 prosecutions in London alone, with magistrates handing out over £1 million in fines.[24]

Without all FPNs being reviewed, which Parliament's Joint Committee on Human Rights has recommended (a proposal rejected by the government),[25] there is no way of knowing how many people were wrongly punished for breaching regulations – innocently caught up in the brute force of the Emergency State.

Do as I say, not as I do

The weather during that first week of lockdown may have been pristinely calm, but the government was swiftly descending into chaos. The day after the lockdown law came into force, the Prime Minister and Health Secretary were diagnosed with COVID-19. Boris Johnson became increasingly ill, until he was admitted to hospital on 9 April. This was a particularly shocking moment which brought home the constitutional chaos accompanying the weirdness of mass quarantine. The legal line of succession should the Prime Minister become incapacitated – that is, who would be in charge of the country – was one of the many issues I had not expected to be commenting on. It later emerged that, while he was isolating for a second time, Johnson had to be barricaded in his office by his staff, who created a 'cat run' between the Downing Street flat and his office so he would not come into contact with colleagues.[26] Meanwhile, Matt Hancock had been hugging and shaking hands with some of my clients shortly before he was diagnosed with COVID-19.[27] These stories at first seemed incongruous. These were the most senior politicians setting pandemic policy, imploring us on nightly broadcasts to take COVID-19 seriously, attempting to conjure up a Blitz spirit. But behind closed doors – and sometimes even in front of the camera, such as when Johnson made a point of shaking hands with hospital staff just as he was advised not to – something was off.[28]

We now know that, by 20 May, Downing Street was hosting a 'bring your own booze' party in the garden for around forty staff, which the Prime Minister attended along with his then fiancée Carrie Symonds. I will discuss 'Partygate' later, in Chapter 8, but it is enough to say at this stage that the Prime Minister broke the rules he imposed on the country, or encouraged others to do so, on multiple occasions during the first year or so of the pandemic. Hancock resigned as Health Secretary the following year, after being exposed for having an extramarital affair with an aide and old friend, Gina Coladangelo. I also believe Hancock was lucky to avoid police investigation and sanction, as I will explain later.

Dominic Cummings, then the Prime Minister's senior adviser, provided another early example of rule-breaking at the heart of government. The Cummings scandal is so well known it even has its own Wikipedia page, so I can state the facts briefly.[29] On 27 March, the same day that the Prime Minister announced he had COVID-19, Cummings' wife was also feeling unwell. Cummings' original version of the story was that he was worried she had COVID-19, and that he would catch it too, and that if they both were ill there would be nobody to look after their four-year-old son. So they got in the car and travelled 264 miles from London to Durham to stay on his parents' estate. The following day he came down with COVID-19. By 12 April, Cummings said he was well enough to return to London. But instead of going straight back, he said, the family drove to Barnard Castle, thirty miles away, to test whether he was well enough to drive, having had problems with his eyesight. On 25 May 2020, after the story had become a national scandal, Cummings gave a press conference from the rather lovely-looking Rose Garden at Downing Street, in what would become one of the defining images of the early pandemic. He gave a quite excruciating account of his reasoning for the various journeys, arguably none of which complied with the regulations that prohibited leaving home except in very limited circumstances. Taking Cummings' explanation at face value, it is possible he left London to 'avoid injury or illness or to escape a risk of harm', a listed reasonable excuse, but it is a stretch. And he gave a wholly different explanation a year later, saying that he had planned on moving to Durham because of threats to his family's security in London.[30] Ironically, this would have been a better explanation, legally speaking. The 'eye-test' trip was less likely to fall within any reasonable excuse. But who knows what to believe? As a lawyer I am used to hearing implausible explanations, and Cummings to me sounded like someone who had been caught and was trying to save some semblance of credibility for himself and the government he represented.

Whatever the truth, the damage had been done. Dr Daisy Fancourt, leading the University College London COVID-19 Social Study, reported that after the Cummings scandal in May 2020, trust in the government to handle the pandemic took a sharp downward turn, and did not recover. The Cummings event was 'pivotal' because it changed the message from 'everyone had to play their part; no excuses, no exemptions', to 'if you could find a loophole in the rules, it somehow became acceptable (and defensible) to break them'. The enemy changed from being the virus itself to 'being the measures designed to curb the virus'.[31] And many people will have felt betrayed not necessarily by the behaviour itself but by the enthusiasm of the government to support Cummings. For many lawyers, the worst part was that the Attorney General had sprung to Cummings' defence, tweeting '[p]rotecting one's family is what any good parent does'.[32] This was a ridiculous thing for the government's law officer to say during a police investigation of a government adviser, but in retrospect it probably indicated how unconcerned the government was about the principle of lawmakers breaking the rules. Later, rule-breaking would come to *define* the government's response to COVID-19. As I write, it is not clear whether there will be the need for more rules, or if we genuinely will now be able to 'live with COVID-19', as the government is hoping. If the latter, then the rift in public trust which opened up due to politicians and officials breaking the rules will be of historic importance. If the pandemic worsens again, and the government has to impose new rules, or some other public health threat emerges, the damage will have real-world consequences.

Pleading for balance

By early April 2020, 3.9 billion people worldwide were locked down. Over ninety countries or territories had asked or ordered their populations to stay at home.[33] In the three months after the first COVID-19 cases were reported in China, state-wide lock-downs had gone from a dystopian fantasy to the daily reality for half the world's population. My focus was on trying to convince anyone who would listen that we needed to take a human rights approach, that is, develop policies which valued, and attempted to balance, basic rights such as the right to life, to family life, to freedom of expression and so on. This was by no means a given. On 31 March, I wrote in the *New Statesman* that:

> Chaos is by definition unpredictable. It is easy, however, to predict how our societies respond to it. We put up walls, close in on ourselves and turn on each other. The modern human rights framework was established after the Second World War precisely because people witnessed how fragile liberal democratic societies are when faced with existential crises.[34]

One of the constant dilemmas I faced during the lockdowns was how to engage constructively with the extraordinary events happening on a daily basis. In the first days of the March 2020 lockdown, I explained in a BBC News interview that the guidance and law differed on how much exercise people were allowed to do each day. That day, I received emails from two different members of the public, variously complaining to my chambers that I had been 'irresponsible' and 'nasty' for telling people 'they're not obliged to follow instructions we've all been given', which were intended, after all, to protect the NHS. One complained to my professional regulator, the Bar Standards Board.[35] Meanwhile, I also began receiving messages and tweets from people who thought lockdown was an egregious and unjustified restriction on liberties. The common refrain I heard more times than I can count was that 'as a human rights lawyer' I should be fighting every aspect of lockdown, which could never be justified.

Particularly in the period when lockdowns were a regular part of life for all of us, I was greatly troubled by this question. What, *as a human rights lawyer*, should I say about lockdowns? The major worldwide human rights organisations were saying that if lockdowns were necessary to implement social distancing, they would be a proportionate response. The United Nations maintained that 'enforced social spacing and social isolation measures . . . if considered necessary and proportionate and evidence-informed, must take into consideration the effects it [*sic*] will have on people and communities and be adapted to ameliorate any negative consequences';[36] though in early April the Secretary-General of the United Nations raised the alarm about the potential negative consequences of locking people in their home, a 'horrifying global surge in domestic violence', tweeting that '[m]any women under lockdown for #COVID19 face violence where they should be safest: in their own homes'.[37]

The Council of Europe's Human Rights Commissioner said that the 'strong measures' being used by European governments were 'necessary to respond to the unprecedented challenge we are facing', but that it was 'crucial' that the authorities take measures that 'do not lead to discrimination and are proportionate to the aims pursued'.[38] And it was clear that there were large sections of society – particularly older people and those with certain underlying health conditions – who were at greater danger from COVID-19. Was it not worth sacrificing – *lending* – others' freedoms for a few months to protect those people while a vaccine was developed?

Experts on healthcare and human rights I spoke to were clear that the rights to life and healthcare would have to, in effect, take precedence over other civil and political rights for a limited period while the 'invisible killer' (to use Boris Johnson's words) was stalking our societies.[39] The WHO's supportive early statements on strong measures from China and then European states continued, for example in October 2020, as the Delta variant was causing havoc around the world and leading states to impose severe new measures: 'although not sustainable – [lockdowns] are needed to swiftly suppress the virus and avoid health systems being overwhelmed'. Lockdowns have 'significant economic, social & broader health impacts', the WHO accepted, and therefore must be 'limited in duration'.[40] But it is notable that the major worldwide human rights organisations followed what appeared to be the general scientific consensus: that lockdowns are sometimes a necessary evil, and generally justified as measures of limited duration which will suppress the virus and 'buy time' while other measures such as contact tracing, increasing healthcare capacity and, ultimately, vaccination are put in place.

I am well aware, and was so at the time, that just because a position appears to have consensus support does not mean it is correct. Extreme social and emotional pressure is a feature of emergencies. This pressure can both clarify and obscure. We can think that the 'answer' to a crisis seems so clear, but that may be as much about the human need to feel that we can control a crisis as identifying the correct solution – the Emergency State is not generally imposed from above, *we want it to happen*. On the other hand, social upheaval can dislodge assumptions which were previously, and wrongly, seen as certainties. Emergencies bring clarity because hard choices, often involving the balancing of essential rights, are taken out of the realm of theoretical musing and into political and social reality.

What to do? I am neither an epidemiologist nor a scientist. As a barrister, I am used to absorbing large amounts of information on diverse topics in a short time. If I am instructed in a case about isolation rules, and it involves scientific evidence, I need properly to understand that evidence before stepping into the court. It could even be said that a key skill for a barrister is giving the *appearance* of expertise in a wide range of areas. But the COVID-19 emergency was something different. It was just so *big*. It enveloped so many parts of society, from science to politics to law. Like a war, everyone had to do their bit to mitigate – even to survive – the upheaval. And in that maelstrom, what role was there for a human rights lawyer? I am used to dealing with particular cases. Sometimes the case will be a vehicle for points of wider principle. But this was different. There were enormous questions in play which had no easy answers.

I tried to look back into history to see if there were better solutions to suppressing, and surviving, a new virus which spread asymptomatically and had no treatment or vaccine. What I found were enforced isolation measures – such as curfews, travel restrictions, gathering bans – going back hundreds if not thousands of years. The logic was clear enough: if you want to stop a virus which spreads by human interaction, you have to limit human interaction, and accept the collateral societal damage. But this did not answer any of the crucial questions about lockdowns that governments worldwide were agonising over: when, for whom, how long for, how severe, and – in legal terms – *how*?

The conclusion I reached was that as a human rights lawyer my efforts would be most usefully spent not pontificating on the huge questions of whether lockdowns could be justified: I could no more reasonably answer that than any other non-scientist. What I did know about was the dangers of emergency laws, and how human rights laws could be used as an early warning system. And as the lockdown began to bite, it became clear that lawyers could play an important role. If you decide to quarantine tens of millions of people using the criminal law, and then fiddle with that law every few days, on average, for two years, it is likely to have some strange effects. One of these was that understanding the law became an essential part of everyday life, and that placed lawyers in an unexpected position. Suddenly, those who were following the lockdown laws – and even claiming to understand them – became gatekeepers to retaining some kind of normalcy.

5. The Lockdown Bites

2 April 2020 to 1 June 2020
Cases: 214,948
Deaths: 33,168
Cumulative deaths: 38,370

By April 2020 it was becoming clear that the police were floundering; theirs was an impossible task made harder by vague powers and law which was inconsistent with government guidance. Having had no warning about becoming public health enforcers, flung well outside their usual comfort zone, and despite the helpful NPCC guidance, some forces were still getting it wrong. Avon and Somerset Police suggested it was against the law for shops to sell non-essential goods and for people not to observe social distancing.[1] Cambridgeshire Police tweeted their approval that 'non essential aisles' in supermarkets were empty, later correcting their mistake and blaming an 'over exuberant officer'.[2]

I made three proposals for policing the pandemic. First, since these were public health not public order powers, the police should focus carefully on the gatherings which were most likely to create a public health risk. Second, individual officers should take responsibility for understanding their powers and ensuring they act proportionately. Third, the police should not encourage people to report each other for breaches of rules because encouraging people to inform on their neighbours could damage social ties and trust.[3]

Yet these issues persisted well beyond the first lockdown. It may be that I had identified the truth of the situation: the police were in an impossible position. A few days later it was reported that police had issued thirty-nine FPNs to children, despite the law only allowing them to be given to people eighteen and over. The FPNs were rescinded following a review.[4]

We don't need no education

Schools remained closed for two and a half months, from 19 March to 1 June 2020, after which a phased reopening began. The schools were not actually obliged by law to close, and they all remained open throughout the pandemic for the relatively small number of children who, for various reasons, such as being the children of 'key workers', were deemed to require in-person teaching. Some schools were quicker than others in transitioning to online education, with some children (including my own) not receiving much until the second time schools were shut, in early 2021. With the exception of the schools that were quick to react, it soon became clear that for some children online education was impossible for lack of access to devices. The reality was that, for many children, online education was a contradiction in terms.

The Human Rights Act includes a right to education.[5] It contains a right not to be discriminated against, also protected by the Equality Act 2010. But, to be blunt, so what? What use are legal rights in the face of the Emergency State? One answer was given by the first coronavirus-related case I acted in, instructed by the Good Law Project, a campaigning organisation.[6] We wrote a pre-action letter to Gavin Williamson, the Secretary of State for Education.[7] This is a formal process where anyone anticipating bringing a legal claim, including against the government, is encouraged to write a letter explaining why they are about to sue. It allows potential parties to tell each other, hopefully in civil terms, what their arguments in court are going to be and possibly save the time and expense of actually bringing the claim by settling the matter, a bit like treating with an enemy before any shots are fired. We wrote to Gavin Williamson explaining that in our view the government was potentially in breach of its legal obligations by failing to provide financial assistance to the one million children estimated as not having adequate access to a device or connectivity at home.[8] We made the point that any issue which disproportionately affects people who are economically worse off is also likely to disproportionately affect Black and minority ethnic communities.

The case never reached court because, on 6 May, the government committed to investing around £85 million in order to provide 200,000 laptops and tablets to disadvantaged families. And despite difficulties sourcing hundreds of thousands of laptops and tablets, by January 2021 the government said that it had provided 700,000 such devices and that over £400 million, paying for 1.3 million laptops, would have been provided by the time the latest tranche of equipment had been delivered.[9] It is possible that this would have happened anyway, given that it did in other countries (this was part of our argument). However, I expect that this case was one of several where the government decided that rather than risk long-winded and costly litigation, it would concede an issue where a sensible suggestion was being made.

This is one reason why it would be wrong to assess the usefulness of human rights and other legal protections according to the cases ultimately won in court, that is, with an all-singing-all-dancing ruling by judges. As with all public law litigation (cases about the legal duties of public authorities), a good case which meets a sensible government lawyer, or even a sensible minister, will be settled. And why should it be otherwise? All parties should be aiming towards the same outcome – ensuring that public authorities comply with their legal obligations. Just as a functioning democracy is in one sense a highly efficient communications system, where useful data makes its way up from the ground to decision-makers, so a case like this, settled early, is a good example of the benefit of human rights and other legal protections.

Trying to protect each other

I kept up my hobby. On 20 April, I was walking through my local park when I came across a man wearing what looked like a repurposed parking attendant uniform, acting as a 'Covid marshal'.[10] A number of marshals were officiously patrolling, looking suspiciously at dog walkers and grass sitters for breaches of the coronavirus regulations. One marshal was speaking to a woman sat alone on a bench. I asked him why he appeared to be berating her, and he responded that he was trying to move her on and that she had been sitting there for half an hour. I pointed out that there was an empty bench next to her and he had no idea what her personal circumstances were. He was civil about it and emphasised that we were all just 'trying to protect each other' and 'work together'. I could not see the point of his actions – what possible public health risk was she posing by sitting on a bench, alone? A few months later, the council closed access to benches by covering them with quarantine tape.

Out of the blue, on 22 April, the government changed the lockdown regulations to make them stricter.[11] It would now be illegal not just to leave your home without a reasonable excuse but to be outside it without one too. Then, on 12 May, forty-seven days after the lockdown had begun, restrictions were relaxed slightly to permit people, in the Prime Minister's words, to 'sit in the sun in your local park . . . drive to other destinations, even play sports, but only with members of your own household'. This was odd because you could probably have done all of those things (except play sport) under the existing law, though the guidance had always been stricter. The key legal change was to allow people to leave and be outside their homes with one other person in order to exercise or for 'open air recreation'. In other words, to sunbathe.[12] Or, as I said when this exception was added to the winter lockdown regulations, to build a snowman.

Lockdowns discriminate

National lockdowns are a superficially simple policy because they impose the same rules on everyone in the country. As the government found out later in 2020, localised restrictions can be targeted at areas with higher case rates but lead to people feeling their area is being unfairly treated. But, in fact, national lockdowns discriminate too.

It is difficult to overstate how *harsh* lockdowns were for many. I sometimes thought of them as a high-stakes game of musical chairs. A person's chances were dictated by the arbitrary fact of where you happened to be standing at the moment the music stopped. So if you happened to be settled in a home with a garden, living with a partner you got on with, and had a job which could be seamlessly transferred from office to Zoom, you would probably be OK. But if you were living in a cramped flat with no outdoor space, or with an abusive partner, or had a job which required you to be in close proximity to people with COVID-19 (such as an ambulance worker who died after contracting COVID-19 in March 2020, and whose family I represented at the inquest into his death), or you were pregnant and had to have your baby with no family support, or had an ill relative in hospital who could not be visited, or you were ill yourself, then you were not so lucky with lockdowns.

Lockdowns also widened social and economic inequalities, particularly among Black and minority ethnic groups. A 2020 study found that Black patients were four times more likely to be infected with COVID-19 than white patients. Similarly, a national study of almost 400,000 people found that people from a Pakistani background were three times more likely to contract the virus than those from a white background.[13] After adjusting for age and geographical region, an increased risk of death was found for Black African (3.24 times) Black Caribbean (2.21 times), Pakistani (3.29 times), Bangladeshi (2.41 times) and Indian (1.70 times) minority ethnic groups.[14]

Why the increased rates of illness and death? A survey by the Runnymede Trust found that one-third of Black and minority ethnic groups (33 per cent) were working outside their home during lockdown, including 41 per cent of Black African groups and 36 per cent of Black Caribbean and Pakistani groups (compared to 27 per cent of white groups).[15] The survey found that more than one-third of Black communities were in key worker roles, with nearly four in ten from Black African groups in front-line key worker employment such as public transport, health and social care (including care workers), teaching (including teaching assistants) and social work. These factors contributed to high exposure to COVID-19, increased stress during lockdowns and dangerous working conditions.

Another study identified the widening of economic and social inequalities along racial lines in several areas.[16] The close-knit nature of many minority ethnic communities (and religious communities in particular) meant that many were left vulnerable to lockdown, and the social isolation that accompanied it had an immense impact on well-being. This was most severely felt by women who faced additional strain from domestic responsibilities. Restrictions on religious gatherings affected all aspects of cultural and family life for many, with burial rites, marriages, births and ordinary worship affected. Participants in the study expressed their communities' struggles with restrictions on social distancing and lockdown measures which had greatly impacted on what would otherwise be high-volume cultural and religious gatherings. The fact that so much information about the pandemic was published digitally meant that those without digital access and skills missed out. Community leaders reported that the pandemic revealed the lack of digital access for their most deprived members. This affected the efficacy of government communications and meant people from minority ethnic communities were less likely to be able to access information about symptoms, treatment and available support.

A Public Health England report found that there was an 'association between belonging to some ethnic groups and the likelihood of testing positive and dying with COVID-19'. The authors were told by stakeholders that racism and discrimination was a root cause 'affecting health, exposure risk and disease progression risk'. Further research was sought on this point in particular.[17] The policing of lockdowns also had a disproportionate impact: Black and minority ethnic people were 54 per cent more likely to be given FPNs than white people.[18] Minority ethnic people were disproportionately subjected to the increased use of force, with 38 per cent of the Metropolitan Police's use of force being applied to Black people, despite Black people making up just 13 per cent of London's population. Further research has underscored the impact that stop and search and harsh policing during the pandemic continues to have on racialised communities in the UK.[19]

While the government mantra of national lockdowns was that we were all in this together, the truth was messier, and more troubling. The bitter reality was that the experience of lockdowns differed radically, and was worse for some groups than others.

The sex ban

Lockdowns had other consequences which I doubt were intended, or expected, by the government – at least at first. If you lived in Leicester from 2020 to 2021, sex indoors with most other people was a criminal offence for 417 days. For the rest of the country, the same applied for substantial periods from 2020 to 2022.

How can these remarkable facts be true? At the end of May 2020, the government withdrew the stay-at-home order. Instead, gatherings of a certain size would be banned. The 'rule of six' would apply to outdoor gatherings. Indoors, it would be illegal to gather with anyone not from your household.[20] The word 'gathering' was also given a definition for the first time: 'when two or more people are present together in the same place in order to engage in any form of social interaction with each other, or to undertake any other activity with each other'. Someone asked me on Twitter whether the rule change meant sex indoors between two people not living together would be illegal. I thought about this. To date, the regulations had had a lot to say about what we did outside our homes, but nothing about what we did inside them. It was illegal to *leave* and *be outside* the home without a reasonable excuse, or to gather *in a public place* with one or more people. But from 1 June it would be just as illegal for me to gather with one other person in my home as it would be to do so in the park, or up a mountain. And since gathering had now been defined as 'any' activity or (somewhat redundantly) 'any form of social interaction' with another, surely sex would count as a gathering, and that meant it would be a crime unless it was between two people who already lived together. A sex ban. I was shocked that this could be the case – how could a criminal law penalise something as basic to human life as sex? And yet, there it was in the increasingly complex regulations which were now coming into force, a sign of the extraordinary reach of the Emergency State.

The news was picked up around the world. *Cosmopolitan* reported the story with the subtitle 'Yup, you read that right'.[21] And although there was a lot of sniggering, it was also very serious. For the next year or so, sex between consenting adults would be a criminal offence in certain parts of the UK if the individuals were not living together or did not fulfill some other limited exception. It is difficult to think of a more severe intrusion into the private lives of people in the UK – this was well beyond the reach even of the severe Second World War regulations. Indeed, this would apply not just to people who met randomly but to long-term partners who did not live together. This was pointed out to the government, which swiftly – well, ten days later, which probably felt like a long time to those waiting – introduced an exception for 'linked households', or 'bubbles' as they would be known colloquially and, confusingly, in government guidance as well. (In passing, I should say that it is baffling why different phrases were used for exactly the same thing – the only reason I can guess at is that the drafters of the law could not bring themselves to use the word 'bubble' in the law of the land.)

On 12 June the regulations were amended to include an exception for people who did not live together to meet, but only if at least one lived alone, so this did not apply, for example, to two students who both lived in separate flat shares.[22] But it demonstrated that the government was responding to public outcries, though in a rather opaque and disjointed way. Again, the government used the emergency procedure under the Public Health Act, which allowed Matt Hancock to bring new regulations into force up to four weeks before they were considered by Parliament, meaning there was no opportunity for

Parliament to consider the fact that sex had been banned between consenting adults, or the linked household 'solution'. And the regulations, with the growing list of exceptions, were starting to look more bloated and confusing – though nothing like what was to come.

I will zip forward in my narrative, briefly, in order to discuss the startling fact that for people in Leicester it was illegal to have sex indoors with someone not from their household or a linked household from 26 March 2020 to 17 May 2021, except for one day.[23] For the rest of the country, it was illegal for at least half of that period. It is probably the case, in fact, that sex between people who did not live together had been illegal from 26 March 2020 when the first lockdown began, as it was illegal to be outside your house without a reasonable excuse, and maintaining a relationship or similar was not included in the list of reasonable excuses. There was a brief window between 13 May and 1 June when you could engage in 'open air recreation' with another, so sex outside was probably permitted in law, although not by social distancing guidance. But from 1 June, the lockdown moved into people's homes, followed by the linked household tweak eleven days later. On 3 July, the limit on indoor gatherings was increased to thirty people in the national regulations.

The following day, local restrictions came into force in Leicester, which was deemed to be a COVID-19 hotspot, meaning that the sex ban was reinstated. From 4 August, the sex ban reappeared in the new local regulations applying to the North of England. Throughout the summer and early autumn, as a patchwork of local restrictions was imposed, the sex ban was switched on and off in various parts of the country. As late as 23 September, six months after the March lockdown, the government released guidance for people in 'established relationships' on whether they should socially distance from each other. It advised, helpfully, that 'you do not need to socially distance . . . from someone you're in an established relationship with'. But this applied only to people who were not subject to local lockdown laws, meaning it applied only to those not already bound by any law requiring them to socially distance indoors.[24] From 3 November 2020, a second national lockdown began, meaning the sex ban was back for everyone until 30 November, when the 'three tiers' system was introduced, segregating the country geographically by different levels of restriction. If you were in one of the stricter tiers, the ban remained in place. But even if the restrictions were looser in your area, this lasted only until the third national lockdown began on 6 January 2021, with the strict indoor gathering restrictions lasting until 17 May 2021.

And so, for residents of Leicester who did not live together and were not part of a linked household, sex indoors was illegal for one year, one month and twenty-one days – 417 days in total. For all other parts of the country, sex was in part illegal for over half of that period, and for some areas, such as Manchester, which only had about a month off from the strictest indoor rules, between 4 July and 8 August 2020, a significant amount more. It is perhaps a feature of our prudish culture that it was treated as a sniggering but not serious criticism of the lockdown rules, during the worst periods of the pandemic. But it was serious for those who were unable to date, or see their partners indoors, or for well over a year had to do so illicitly, risking an FPN or criminal conviction, because of blunt and disproportionate legal restrictions. This did not apply in many other European countries, which permitted people to visit each other, one at a time, even during the strictest lockdowns.[25] And despite urgent appeals from the many affected, nothing except the linked household exception was done to make things a bit more manageable for people.[26]

There is perhaps no better illustration of the absurdity of this rule than the fact that Matt Hancock, the Health Secretary throughout the lockdowns, and whose name was quite literally at the end of almost all of the myriad regulations, ultimately resigned because he was caught engaging in an extramarital affair with an aide at work, when they were pictured kissing and clinching on the front page of the *Sun*. On 26 June 2021, Hancock claimed he was resigning for 'breaking the guidance', but it remains my view that he most likely broke the law too. This is because for much of the pandemic it was not possible, legally, to be in a physical relationship with someone not from your household, and neither qualified to be the other's linked household as neither lived alone.[27] Both parties were fortunate that at the time the Metropolitan Police Service (the Met) said it would not investigate Hancock over alleged breaches of Covid regulations because it did not look into Covid-related issues retrospectively 'as a matter of course',[28] though a few months later, as a result of a judicial review I acted in relating to Partygate, the Met publicly was forced to reveal its full policy on whether to investigate offences retrospectively, a policy it had referred to internally as being for people with a 'high public profile'.[29] Assuming that Hancock conducted an affair in the workplace, and perhaps elsewhere, it is hard to see how the Met could have avoided investigating had its 'high public profile' policy been public knowledge. Matt Hancock personally signed the very laws he potentially broke. The failure of the Met even to investigate him surely undermined the legitimacy of the law, one of the criteria which, under the Met's policy, should have required them to investigate.

In the meantime, many thousands of people were unable to develop or maintain basic human relationships. Who knows how many relationships failed as a result, or never sparked into life? A testament to the immense impact of the Emergency State, and its unprecedented reach.

6. Patchwork Summer

2 June 2020 to 1 September 2020
Cases: 84,840
Deaths: 3,325
Cumulative deaths: 41,695

Just as the first lockdown was being relaxed, the reach of the coronavirus regulations was rapidly expanding. This would herald a summer of attempts to micromanage local restrictions, inconsistent messaging, and arguing over whether we should be 'eating out to help out' or staying in to avoid another wave. Meanwhile, the coronavirus laws would be added to and tinkered with on an almost daily basis, leading to mass confusion and significant expansion of the Emergency State.

On 3 June 2020, a new set of travel regulations appeared, requiring most people arriving in England to self-isolate.[1] These regulations were significant as they marked the first time there would be a legal requirement for anyone to self-isolate, though it would have been more accurate to describe this as quarantine – these were generally *not* people who were suspected of having COVID-19. Surprisingly, the law requiring anyone to self-isolate if they had COVID-19 would not appear until September 2020. Then, from 15 June, a new law mandated face coverings on public transport. It would be a criminal offence to disobey, though this would be enforced first with a Fixed Penalty Notice.[2] Both of these policies seemed sensible. The requirement for travellers to quarantine was a policy which probably should have been in place much earlier, given the obvious risk in the early days of the pandemic from people arriving from places where COVID-19 was more established. The requirement to wear a face covering would generate fearsome debate in some quarters, but it was at the least a rational policy, based on the evidence presented to the government by its advisory group.[3] The controversy was in fact not new: face-covering mandates in the United States during the 1918 influenza pandemic were so controversial that a public health official in San Francisco shot a man who refused to put on a mask.[4]

A troubling aspect of the ballooning rules was that the government continued to use the emergency procedure which allowed regulations to come into force with no vote in Parliament until four weeks later. Events were moving so quickly that often the debate did not happen (because it was by that time redundant), or was academic by the time it took place (because the policy had already been eased). And because all of the coronavirus restrictions were brought in using secondary legislation, Parliament had no opportunity to amend them. So, for example, the quarantine rules for incoming travellers were so strict they were similar to house arrest. They were arguably even more severe than the conditions ordered by courts to restrict the movements of offenders released from prison on licence. Recent travellers were not even permitted to leave home for exercise, and could only leave the house for emergency purposes. This applied not because someone was infected, or because they had come into contact with an infected person, but simply because they had been in another country: on any view, an extraordinary and unprecedented use of quarantine powers to apply to such a wide group. There was no distinction made between countries with varying COVID-19 rates; everyone who arrived had to be subjected to effective house arrest. By 3 June, some travellers were arriving from places where there was *less* chance of being infected with COVID-19 than in the UK itself. And yet the new travel regulations appeared five days before they came into force on 8 June. As far as I can find, this severe restriction on liberty was never even debated in Parliament. The face-covering regulations were debated for *twenty-five minutes* in committee on 6 July.[5]

To an extent, it is possible to excuse the lack of debate and the use of the emergency procedure in the first few weeks of the pandemic. It was not obvious that Parliament would even be able to operate in person or through some kind of hybrid arrangement. But after the first few weeks it was obvious enough that Parliament was being sidelined. Tom Hickman QC, a law professor and barrister, raised the troubling legal implications of using a vaguely worded statutory instrument to lock down the population.[6] I suggested that it was possible to make good laws during a bad pandemic, but that there was a 'scrutiny vacuum', 'which, as the emergency goes on for weeks, months, perhaps even years, becomes ever-less defensible'.[7] I proposed that although emergency laws may be necessary, they should still satisfy four tests. First, they must be scrutinised by Parliament. Second, they must be lawful, in the sense that they must be strictly within the boundaries of the powers granted by the Public Health Act. Third, they must be impermanent – the threat could persist but 'we must jealously guard our liberties and ensure they are restricted for as long as is necessary and not a moment more'. Finally, they must be proportionate – that is, they should be as close as possible to the precise restrictions necessary to contain COVID-19. Unfortunately, the final test is not one which was easy to apply to the COVID-19 pandemic, because information was usually incomplete. But that was *why* scrutiny was so important – not because of an unrealistic ideal of perfect democracy but because democracy works by exposing important decisions to the fire of public debate. Some of the policy decisions would doubtless have been quite different, and better, had scrutiny been allowed and Parliament not reduced to a 1,400-person rubber stamp.

There is an irony to the fact that in September 2019, just as the COVID-19 pandemic was about to begin, the Supreme Court ruled against the attempt by Boris Johnson's government to shut down Parliament to avoid debate over its Brexit deal. And yet, just a few months later, the government's use of the emergency Public Health Act powers would in effect do just that. And as this went on not for months but for years, Parliament became so used to its diminished role that it effectively prorogued itself.

The purgatory of local lockdowns

The basic freedoms people in England enjoyed during the summer and early autumn of 2020 were for many a literal postcode lottery. From July to October, twenty-nine different laws were brought into force, all using the emergency procedure, so without prior debate in Parliament. The government's strategy was to avoid national lockdown by calibrating the rules in every part of England depending on the rate of COVID-19 infections. But this approach brought its own problems. From a harsh but relatively simple eleven-page law applying to the whole of England, the public were suddenly faced with a patchwork of restrictions. Each new law included a list of postcodes where the rules would apply, and even individual addresses where 'part of a postcode district is in the protected area'. For example, in the Leicester lockdown rules – the first to use this approach – Nos. 209 and 211 Glen Road in Oadby were included in the lockdown, while the rest of the street was not. How the other residents, including those in lucky No. 208, avoided the lockdown was unexplained.

Even more worryingly, although the Leicester lockdown was announced on 30 June, the regulations were not published until four days afterwards.[8] Local people and businesses would have to rely on guesswork for four days to know what behaviour constituted a criminal offence and which non-essential businesses were to close. Meanwhile, *The Times* reported that police would carry out spot checks on vehicles leaving the Leicester area, to ensure residents were complying with the local lockdown.[9] How, when they had no powers in law to enforce the lockdown yet, was anybody's guess.[10] Leicester's lockdown eased a little in early August, but not in time for Eid al-Adha, an important Muslim festival. It appeared then that the timing was deliberate, as the festival would involve significant household mixing.[11]

Parts of the UK, particularly many in the North, never really emerged from lockdown. As the South celebrated pubs reopening on 4 July (no doubt the Prime Minister enjoyed the significance of the 'independence day' date), and children including my own enjoyed the playgrounds which were open for the first time since March, much of the North was quickly plunged into further lockdowns which for many would last almost another year. In Leicester, severe restrictions lasted 417 days. In Manchester, the UK's third-largest city, residents were released from severe restrictions for only four weeks of those 417 days.

During this period, the lockdown laws became more complex and unpredictable. Local lockdowns followed for Blackburn (with Darwen) and Luton on 24 July;[12] Bradford, Greater Manchester, Lancashire and West Yorkshire on 4 August;[13] the Greencore Food to Go factory in Northampton, where there had been a COVID-19 outbreak, on 29 August (without doubt the most local of local lockdowns attempted);[14] Bradford again on 7 September;[15] Bolton on 10 September;[16] Birmingham, Sandwell and Solihull on 14 September;[17] and most of the North-East of England on 17 September.[18] And I have only mentioned the introduction of the lockdowns – there were also multiple tweaks to each local lockdown, to open or close businesses and give people slightly more, or less, freedom to gather. It truly was a summer of micromanaging, and difficult bordering on impossible for the public to follow the swiftly changing rules.

Dog law and the £10,000 Fixed Penalty Notice

While the North entered new local lockdowns, in the South, the government was actively encouraging indoor socialising with the 'Eat Out to Help Out' scheme, giving a 50 per cent government-funded discount at restaurants.[19] Somewhat incongruously, it was also cracking down on gatherings of more than thirty people in a private dwelling, and raves. For anyone who grew up in the 1990s, the focus on the social 'evil' of rave culture was a throwback, but it was unsurprising that illegal raves were making a comeback given the absence of indoor clubs or summer festivals. Anyone caught holding, or being 'involved in the holding of', such gatherings would be given an FPN of £10,000, an eye-watering amount and a 5,000 per cent increase on the FPN of £200 for a minor offence.[20]

Perhaps the first recipient of a £10,000 FPN was Piers Corbyn, the brother of the former Labour leader Jeremy Corbyn, and an anti-lockdown campaigner. He received it for organising a protest rally which took place on 29 August, the day after the new regulations came into force. He was also detained for ten hours.[21] Although Piers Corbyn was responsible for spreading dangerous COVID-19 conspiracy theories, I was uncomfortable with that FPN. The law had only changed the previous day and it was not trailed in advance by the government – or at least not in the expansive form we saw on 28 August – it was meant to be focused on raves. After I read the law, I suggested that it would apply to children's birthday parties as much as it did to raves, the stated aim of the policy, and that 'being involved in the holding' of a gathering was very wide language which could include buying a cake for the birthday party. But it is not clear to what extent Corbyn or anyone else who received £10,000 FPNs for the 29 August rally knew any of this. One of the dangers of fast-changing, confusing and essentially inaccessible law-making is that it becomes a 'dog law', a 1792 phrase of philosopher Jeremy Bentham's:

> It is the judges (as we have seen) that make the common law. Do you know how they make it? Just as a man makes laws for his dog. When your dog does anything you want to break him of, you wait till he does it, and then beat him for it. This is the way you make laws for your dog: and this is the way the judges make law for you and me. They won't tell a man beforehand what it is he *should not do* – they won't so much as allow of his being told: they lie by till he has done something which they say he should not *have done*, and then they hang him for it.[22]

I am sure that the COVID-19 pandemic gave rise to many instances of dog law, where people were so hopelessly confused by the ever-changing regulations that they inadvertently breached them. It is trite to say that ignorance of the law is no defence. But that is not the end of the story. Sometimes a law is so unclear, or impossible for a person to know, that it becomes *unfair* to enforce it.

In human rights law, a law must be accessible and predictable enough to comply with the requirement of 'no punishment without law'.[23] For example, the European Court of Human Rights has said that a court order mandating someone to be of 'good behaviour' was so vague that it breached their rights to freedom of expression.[24] The same protection exists in English common law. But throughout the pandemic, people were punished with FPNs and even criminal prosecutions under vague laws which changed, on average, more than once per week.[25] This is not to say that every FPN or prosecution was unfair. But it has been shown by the Crown Prosecution Service's own reviews that many FPNs should not have been given and many prosecutions should never have been instigated.

Protesting lockdown

There was a second reason Piers Corbyn's FPN was interesting. At the time, no more than thirty people could gather outdoors unless the gathering fell within an exception. A new exception had been added on 4 July for protest, but only if the protest fulfilled certain conditions, the most onerous of which was that the organisers take all reasonable measures to limit the risk of transmission of the virus, taking into account both the risk assessment and government guidance. A feature of the Emergency State is that usual lines of communication between the public and decision-makers tend to be cut off, which makes it even more important that the public have the opportunity to communicate directly with those in charge through protest. But during much of the pandemic, protest was treated as illegal. Even during the brief periods when the protest exception was in place, once the £10,000 FPN was introduced the risk of failing to conduct an adequate risk assessment became far greater. I was contacted during the summer of 2020 by a number of organisations who were so concerned at putting their own organisers at risk of a £10,000 FPN that they decided not to go ahead.[26] There was no formal process for police to pre-approve risk assessments, meaning the law looked a lot like a dog law, or at least one which was so vague it had a chilling effect on protest. If the police's interpretation of the coronavirus regulations was wrong, as it later turned out to have been on occasion, the implication was that much of the policing of protest during the pandemic was itself unlawful.

The anti-lockdown protests were an important way for people to oppose lockdown measures. The reason protesters were often penalised, even when the rules allowed some protests, was that many would not comply with the requirement that a protest would be permitted only if government guidance was followed. They were caught out by their refusal on principle to wear face coverings, for example, or socially distance. Some might say anti-lockdown protesters were hoisted with their own petard. But this does at least show that there is no single idea of 'freedom'. We all prioritise different freedoms. It is up to the state to mediate between different conceptions of what it is to be free, and sometimes one group will be prioritised over another. During the pandemic, when protest was permitted, it was in effect illegal to protest against social distancing and face coverings if you refused to practise those safety measures at the protest itself – and I imagine most would agree this is a reasonable balance to have struck.

The philosopher John Stuart Mill said that the only purpose for which power can be rightfully exercised over any member of a civilised community against their will is to prevent harm to others.[27] But that begs the question as to what harm, exactly, is being prevented. Many would see the effective ban on anti-lockdown protests as a proportionate restriction on the right to protest, given that COVID-19 was so infectious, with no vaccine available at that time, and the fact any large non-socially distanced gathering could be a super-spreader event – even if it was outdoors.[28] Ultimately, compelled social distancing was premised on it being too costly to society at large, for a limited period, to trust people to make their own choices based only on guidance.

One of the most important questions to resolve before the next pandemic is whether a guidance-based system, without the criminal law being involved at all, would have worked. Because there are two important arguments against restrictions on protest – and indeed many other social activities – even during the worst periods of 2020. First, although social distancing and face coverings might be sensible guidance, it is not for the state to compel individuals to follow it. If a group of people who are all against social distancing and face coverings want to congregate, unmasked and un-distanced, for the purpose of protest, is it really for the state to tell them not to? Some might approve of this argument, based on the freedom to choose – and even to make mistakes – being as important as any other freedom. For a second argument, we can again cite John Stuart Mill, but in the opposite direction. Mill emphasised the importance of free discussion in ensuring we get things right in the end. 'Complete liberty of contradicting and disproving our opinion', he said, 'is the very condition which justifies us in assuming its truth for purposes of action.' A person's judgement is only deserving of confidence because 'he has kept his mind open to criticism of his opinions and conduct' – a principle which surely applies to governments too.[29]

But the argument which critics of restrictions never fully grappled with was that a choice not to comply with social distancing had consequences not just for the individual doing the choosing but for society at large. In a society where a deadly virus is spreading, we are all potential transmitters of infection and the risks we take have consequences for *others*, and some of those others will be far more vulnerable to the virus than we are. The consequences of our actions are not just personal, they are *social*. When faced with a pandemic, individual rights must go alongside, and be balanced with, collective responsibilities. And so, while outdoor protest should not have been in effect banned, I also believe it was reasonable to make social distancing and other mitigating measures a condition of it. After all, during a pandemic, one person's freedom could be another's death sentence.

7. The Darkest Winter

2 September 2020 to 31 January 2021
Cases: 3,573,188
Deaths: 68,790
Cumulative deaths: 110,485

During the summer of 2020, many hoped that COVID-19 was in retreat. The government encouraged socialising to get the economy back on track, as if the shock was over and it was time to recover. Unsurprisingly, hope alone would not protect against a still-new virus which had infected only a small percentage of the population, with the rest remaining as unprotected as they were in March 2020. The vaccination was making progress but not yet ready to inject hope into arms, as Matt Hancock tended to put it. But few imagined that the winter of 2020–21 would be so brutal, with 60,000 dead and over three million new cases. The government, meanwhile, seemed to swing between false reassurance, misplaced optimism and panicky measures imposed at the last possible moment and symbolised by the constant changes to the increasingly complicated coronavirus regulations.

By early September 2020, case rates were rising and the government began to tighten national restrictions again. On 14 September, the 'rule of six' was reintroduced for all gatherings.[1] As had become the norm, the regulations – which made complex amendments to both the national and local lockdowns – arrived so late that Parliament could not consider them in advance and the public were left casting about for explanation; it was a bad sign when many, including the police, were relying on my

Twitter feed rather than official sources. This was a particularly egregious example of late publication, with the regulations appearing twenty minutes before they came into force at 12:01 a.m. on 14 September. The police were so blindsided that the Chair of the National Police Federation resorted to begging on national television for more guidance.[2] Parliament's Public Administration and Constitutional Affairs Committee, not known for publishing anti-government screeds, said in mid-September that the case for using the urgent procedure in the Public Health Act, particularly for regulations *easing* lockdown – which, after all, could have been predicted – had not always been justified, and that the government should 'accord greater priority to scheduling debates on such legislation in a timelier manner'.[3] But the government was not listening: the practice continued for the remainder of 2020, and indeed into 2021 and 2022.

This and other issues were raised in a major cross-Parliamentary and cross-party Joint Committee on Human Rights (JCHR) report which I had been working on as Specialist Adviser.[4] The JCHR plays a vital role in scrutinising a range of human rights issues, but this inquiry was different: instead of reviewing an issue in retrospect, the COVID-19 inquiry would analyse the lockdown restrictions in real time. Over the course of a year, the inquiry would produce six detailed reports, covering the huge range of human rights issues which the lockdown was causing, from the right to family life being demolished to the right to protest being practically extinguished for the first time in British history. The September 2020 report raised a host of issues which had been evident since the first weeks of lockdown: ambiguity and mixed messaging by ministers, the discrepancy between guidance and law and the growing problem of public understanding, noting that at the end of July under half (45 per cent) of people in England had a 'broad understanding' of the current lockdown rules, compared to 90 per cent across the UK during the strict lockdown period.[5]

Perhaps trying to address that point, the Prime Minister had said that the new gathering restrictions would be 'simplified'; but when they were finally published, just the part on gatherings had ballooned from 825 to over 2,000 words, with a range of new exceptions. They included a new rule which allowed large indoor events to continue if they complied with social distancing requirements and people attended as household groups or as a maximum of six people – while not, however, being permitted to 'mingle' with other household groups. It was not obvious what that meant and government ministers were left floundering when asked. And the public weren't alone in being confused. The Home Secretary, Priti Patel, who had signed the new regulations into law, told BBC Radio 4's *Today* programme that a family of four stopping and chatting to another family of four on the way to the park would be 'mingling' and therefore committing a criminal offence, which was itself wrong – the rule against mingling only applied to certain indoor events. Are you following? If not, you would have been in good company.

The banality of corruption

There was another curiosity about the new regulations, a new exception for a 'relevant outdoor activity'. This was defined as:

> a physical activity which is carried on outdoors and for which a licence, permit or certificate issued by a public body . . . to carry on the activity, or for any of the equipment used for the purposes of the activity, must be held by (a) the gathering organiser, or (b) any person taking part in the activity.

But what activities would fall within this innocuous-sounding exception? As it happens, grouse shooting and hunting, the activities it was expressly, and secretly, designed to permit.

It was reported on the Monday the regulations came into force that the Cabinet Office's special COVID-19 Operations ministerial committee – chaired by then Cabinet Office Minister Michael Gove – had scheduled a meeting on the previous Saturday, with one agenda item: 'Exemption: hunting and shooting'. The meeting was cancelled at short notice, with cabinet ministers and officials told that the issue would be discussed later. The *Huffington Post* reported that insiders believed the meeting was axed to avoid any ministers raising objections. Instead, the 'outdoor activity' wording was inserted in the regulations. One source said the entire issue held up the publication of the regulations until shortly before the new law was due to come into force at midnight on Sunday.[6] Civil servants were up late into the night, having been instructed to conceal the purpose of the exception in innocent-sounding wording. Dominic Cummings, the Prime Minister's adviser at the time, revealed to me that he was driving on the Sunday when the Prime Minister asked for a conference call between him and the Covid Task Force: 'we gotta exempt grouse shooting or the [members of Parliament] will go crackers . . . argh getting loads of incoming on grouse shooting, argh chief [whip] says it's bad we're gonna have to fold on this one yeah i know it sounds crazy'. Cummings described himself as punching the steering wheel and shouting 'no no no no NOOOOOOO', concerned that the policy would be 'Wednesbury unreasonable' – that is, open to legal challenge because it is a decision no reasonable person would ever make.[7]

This anecdote is colourful but it also illustrates an important point. The political philosopher and Holocaust survivor Hannah Arendt coined the expression 'the banality of evil' when describing Adolf Eichmann, a senior bureaucrat for the Nazi genocide of Jews, who claimed he was doing his duty because he was following orders and obeying laws. Arendt's phrase has become emblematic of the tendency of institutions to become corrupt under a veneer of process and hierarchy. Corruption has been defined by Transparency International as the 'abuse of public power for private benefit'.[8] In the Emergency State, public power becomes highly concentrated, and often held by a few individuals in the government. Meanwhile, the usual safeguards against misbehaviour, such as scrutiny by the legislature and courts, and the healthy mistrust the public ordinarily have for those in power, are diminished. This is a heady cocktail for those who suddenly and unexpectedly find they have almost godlike power over others' lives, as well as over the country's resources. I doubt that in these situations ministers and public officials are necessarily seeking personal gain. But once it becomes clear that you are exercising serious power, the petitioning will begin in earnest: friends, family, donors, people who happen to have your WhatsApp details because they own a pub behind your house – requests will come from all sides.

Imagine the scene: you are a relatively junior official who suddenly finds themselves in a meeting with the Prime Minister and ten others deciding which businesses will open and which will shut, who will leave the house and who will stay at home, which children will go to school and which will be 'home schooled', whether a sport will be legal, if people will be allowed to worship . . . This is *too much power* for any one person or small group. And yet those were the decisions being made at the Covid Operations Cabinet Committee meetings throughout the pandemic.

The decisions which would shape tens of millions of lives more than any in recent history were in fact being made by a group of four ministers – in 2020–21, the Prime Minister Boris Johnson, Chancellor Rishi Sunak, Cabinet Office Minister Michael Gove and Health Secretary Matt Hancock. A few other key officials responsible for COVID-19 policy would join too.[9] There were no minutes published for these meetings – though there were for SAGE meetings and almost every other significant meeting. All the public saw was the metaphorical white smoke which appeared at the end of the meeting in the form of new regulations which would set the boundaries of people's everyday lives. And since no minutes were published, it was impossible to trace the origins of a particular policy idea to any particular individual. This is a recipe for corruption of the kind seen with the grouse shooting exception. It would have been one thing to include an exception for grouse shooting and justify it in Parliament – there is nothing corrupt about admitting it has been added to please your party's MPs, though you may end up in political trouble. What is corrupt is responding to private lobbying by cancelling a planned meeting and instructing civil servants to work late to create an exception which will *conceal* its purpose and therefore its origin.

It also sparks some important questions – was this an exception or the norm? Was this the only occasion that private lobbying led to a change in a lockdown law? What other motivations may have been at play when making decisions which not only would dictate our social lives, but at the stroke of a minister's pen could also wipe millions from, or add millions to, the value of a business or business sector?

I asked Dominic Cummings whether there were other examples of the rules being skewed by private lobbying. He responded cryptically, 'loads, mainly tory mps, carrie [the Prime Minister's then fiancée and now wife], or the telegraph'. He went on to give a specific example of 'direct bungs' to the newspapers, negotiated directly with the Prime Minister with no officials on the calls and dressed up as 'covid relief'.[10] The story related to a subsidy paid to large press organisations since the beginning of the pandemic, and involved a huge amount of public money – £35 million intended for the first three months, followed by an unknown amount in the following twenty months.[11] The details of the scheme remain murky.

Then there was the £7.9 billion spent on personal protective equipment (PPE) during the procurement bonanza in the first months of the pandemic. Anyone who has followed Jolyon Maugham QC's Good Law Project's litigation relating to the issue will have at the least felt disquiet at the 'VIP lane' set up to give priority access to personal contacts of MPs, Lords and officials, and at the inflated prices paid for equipment and the lack of transparency from the government. In total, £3.9 billion worth of contracts were awarded through the VIP lane.[12] The National Audit Office has reported that 46 out of the 115 contracts awarded via the VIP lane did not go through a detailed due diligence process, so the government 'was not in a position to fully understand the contract management risks it was exposing itself to with some of these suppliers'. The government has argued that these factors in combination are not evidence of corruption, but of the unprecedented demand in the world markets for PPE caused by the pandemic, and the need to cut some of the usual procurement red tape in order to secure the many billions of items we needed.

Yet some of the stories, particularly of the VIP lane, remain troubling. While Matt Hancock was Health Secretary, and therefore in charge of NHS procurement, his ex-neighbour and local pub landlord, who had no previous experience in manufacturing PPE, secured the benefit of a £40-million PPE contract after sending Hancock a WhatsApp message. Hancock attempted to deny the story by telling Parliament that 'the man in question never got nor applied for a contract from the government or the NHS at all'. But this was a half-truth. The ex-neighbour's company was subcontracted by another supplier, and Hancock had referred him to an official, a fact that only came to light after a freedom of information request by the *Guardian*.[13] Other bizarre-sounding contracts have been revealed, such as £108 million to a small pest-control company, and the same amount to a confectioner in Northern Ireland. The courts have found that VIP contracts were not published by the government in sufficient time.[14] And we also know that record-keeping was poor – Tom Sasse, from the Institute for Government, told the BBC that '[t]he Cabinet Office did not manage to keep a proper account of who recommended a particular supplier, which opens it up to accusations of cronyism'.[15]

Court challenges to decisions to use 'no competition' emergency procurement have, to date, mostly failed.[16] But the potential for abuse of the extraordinarily lax procurement system, in combination with the VIP lane that gave an advantage to those with personal connections, created a huge risk of corruption. This is a classic risk of the Emergency State, with the usual anti-corruption safeguards removed and a few individuals given huge power of patronage. It seems, from the way ministers have defended passing on 'leads' for PPE, that they believed they were doing what was best for the country by ensuring there was enough PPE. But when the good of the country becomes synonymous with the good of a minister's pals (or pub landlord), the conditions become ripe for corruption. The VIP lane may have brought in a few more masks, but the cost was the corrosion of trust that the state benefits the public not the private interests of those in power. It begins with the relative banality of grouse shooting, but where does it stop?

Ending in tiers

The lockdown regulations were expanding horizontally, in girth, but also vertically, in number, with new requirements from 18 September 2020 for certain businesses to take personal details for contract tracing and to display a QR code for people to scan.[17] On 28 September, it became a legal requirement, for the first time, to isolate if you tested positive for COVID-19 or to quarantine if you were told by the NHS that you had come into close contact with a positive case.[18]

On 17 October, it was reported that police were to be given access to NHS Test and Trace data.[19] This was undoubtedly a significant expansion of the Emergency State, with police being given the keys, for the first time, to an individual's health data so they would know if someone had been told to quarantine or isolate. It was also a natural consequence of the self-isolation rules: how could the police enforce them without knowing who was subject to them? But it was still another step change in the relationship between the police and the public, and in the corrosion of the right to privacy.

Meanwhile, the lockdown regulations were becoming increasingly complex. Linked childcare households (childcare bubbles) were added to permit informal childcare arrangements.[20] On 30 September, new rules were introduced for the North of England, where six people would be permitted in pubs if they did not mingle. Remarkably, singing in a group of two or more people was banned in the North of England only. I found myself explaining through emojis on Twitter that karaoke in the South was limited to six people (because of the rule of six), but that in the North only solo karaoke was allowed indoors, and singing in a group of no more than six outdoors.[21]

Each of these exceptions made sense from a scientific and social perspective – singing, for example, projected droplets which could spread COVID-19. Millions needed informal childcare, and the previous rules had outlawed this. But the costs of more exceptions, allowing for more of the vagaries of human life, were simplicity and public understanding. The government was behaving like an app developer who obsessively tinkers with the interface, leaving users increasingly baffled. Perhaps this approach indicated the government's mixed feelings about the restrictions – on the one hand, they were broadly necessary to slow the spread of a deadly virus; on the other, those in power could not resist the temptation to blunt their edges. The problem was that less harsh measures might not be effective enough to justify the immense impact on freedom, or may be required for a longer period, as evidenced by the lockdown purgatory which large parts of England experienced from March 2020 to May 2021. Like a guest at the Hotel California, the North of England could check out of lockdown but never leave.

The government's solution to the confusion over the ballooning local restrictions was to rebrand. Instead of bespoke restrictions for identified towns and postcodes, there would now be three 'tiers' of rules. Parliament was, however, finally becoming restive about being sidelined over rule changes. MPs objected ever more loudly in the media and in the House. Kieran Mullan, MP for Crewe and Nantwich, said the government needed to do more to explain the rationale behind its policies if it expected people to follow the rules. 'If we don't have the confidence and faith of the public in national measures,' he said, 'we've got very little chance of getting them to listen to us on local measures . . . If [MPs] can't explain them, what chance have we got of doing that successfully?'[22] The pressure told, and the government permitted Parliament a vote on the new tiers regulations before they came into force. In the context of the previous seven months, this was revolutionary, but still thin gruel. The ninety-two pages of new law, with Goldilocks-style medium, high and very high levels, were published just after 6 p.m. on Monday 12 October, in order to be debated and voted in on Tuesday, and to come into force on Wednesday.[23] As usual, Parliament was not able to suggest changes, so the vote would be for a simple 'yes' or 'no'. And despite rising discontent, there was nothing like a majority of Parliamentarians willing to derail the entire train and be blamed for rising COVID-19 deaths. The debate and vote were in essence a sham, even if they made MPs feel a bit better about *appearing* to do their job of holding government to account.

One benefit of the three tiers was that, for the first time, the opaque decision-making was not about the kind of restrictions but about where they would apply as the different levels of restrictions were now known in advance. For a brief period, the public were not wondering whether they would be subject to unexpected new rules, but instead whether their area would be plunged into a higher tier.

Suddenly, local mayors became involved: *You aren't going to put my area into the pub-closing tier!* Most prominently, Andy Burnham, the Labour Mayor of Greater Manchester, entered into fractious negotiations with the government. Burnham demanded more financial support if Manchester was put into Tier 3, the 'very high' level, though ultimately the government walked away from talks and, on 23 October, put Manchester into Tier 3 anyway. It was notable that this was probably the most high-profile attempt to wrest some control of lockdown decision-making away from the small cabal within Downing Street.[24] But the government's response was a power play and a message to other local mayors that there was no point attempting to do the same. The harsh reality was that the government had all the power it needed and local mayors had precious little leverage beyond influencing public opinion. And what difference would public opinion make if MPs were not playing any substantive role in the passing of lockdown laws? As spirited as his objection was, Andy Burnham might as well have been screaming into the void.

The second national lockdown

The three tiers lasted just twenty-two days before rising case and death rates caused the government to sweep them away, replacing them with a national lockdown which came into force on Bonfire Night, 5 November 2020.[25]

The second lockdown would be significantly different to the first, and much less strict. Schools would remain open, and there were now a large range of exceptions, including being able to exercise with one other person. Another exception was that outdoor events of any scale would be permitted on Remembrance Sunday. Meanwhile, the exception for socially distanced outdoor protests had been removed. This contrast demonstrates well the priorities of the government – and that it believed unlimited outdoor events *could* be safe, but would be permitted only if they were important enough to the government. Priti Patel, the Home Secretary, was said to have been directly responsible for the removal of the protest exception, perhaps swayed by the fact that anti-lockdown protests were happening throughout Europe, including in London. The Home Office noted the right to peaceful protest being 'the cornerstone of our democracy', but said that 'any gathering risks spreading the disease, leading to more deaths'.[26] And so protest was banned, apparently on the direction of the Home Secretary. Or was it? The High Court would be forced to answer that question a few months later.

'Hard-hitting emotional messaging'

By mid-October, as the more infectious Alpha variant took hold and death rates were rising quickly, many, including the

Labour leader Keir Starmer, had been calling for a 'circuit breaker' two-week national lockdown.[27] The Prime Minister did not follow the advice. Instead, two weeks later, he instituted a national lockdown limited to twenty-eight days.[28] But as December loomed, it was looking like this would be no ordinary Christmas. On 21 November, Lord Sumption wrote in the *Daily Mail*:

> Understandably, many people believe the only thing that matters will be the risk of death or serious illness . . . for many others, there will be a range of values in play which are at least as important: family, love and companionship, human contact, generosity of spirit, beauty and spontaneous joy. The question is not which group is right. It is whether we should be allowed to make the choice for ourselves, instead of having it imposed on us by law . . . But for the Jacobins of [SAGE] and the control freaks in the Department of Health, theirs is the only answer. This is because they are interested only in death, whereas the rest of us are more interested in life.[29]

Sumption also raised the spectre of deliberate fearmongering by the government. He highlighted a 22 March SAGE document, published just before the first lockdown, which, under the heading 'persuasion', included the line: 'The perceived level of personal threat needs to be increased among those who are complacent, using hard-hitting emotional messaging.'[30] This is what the government had done, Sumption argued, and 'in scaring the public, it has also limited its options, because it has had to live up to its own doom-laden narrative'. The SAGE line was regularly cited by those arguing against lockdown restrictions, and became something of a meme.[31] It was used to explain the argument that SAGE and the government were trumping up the risks of COVID-19 in order to justify restrictions which were not necessary to contain a relatively benign virus. As I read Lord Sumption's arguments now, with the benefit of distance from a truly frightening period, the essential point which he had been making since the first days of the lockdown remains a powerful one. It is not obvious that our government – or governments worldwide – got the balance right between guidance and compulsion. Lockdowns slowed but never stopped the spread of COVID-19. And it is undoubtedly the case that deploying the full power and force of the state to compel people fundamentally to alter their social and working lives did collateral damage: to our basic rights to make decisions about the risks and benefits of everyday activities, to our relationship with state authority, and to our democracy, which was partly suspended for two years. There may even be lasting harm to the state itself, with politicians and public authorities becoming addicted to the drug of law by decree and to deep incursions into our private lives.

But was the state really deliberately trumping up the threat of COVID-19? As any lawyer knows, it is always worth checking the full text. The oft-used text was not from SAGE itself but its behavioural science subgroup, SPI-B, for discussion at SAGE's next monthly meeting. The point being made was that a 'substantial number of people still do not feel sufficiently personally threatened', perhaps because 'they are reassured by the low death rate in their demographic group'. The sentence about 'hard-hitting emotional messaging' was followed by the qualification that for this to be effective it 'must also empower people by making clear the actions they can take to reduce the threat'. The paper went on to say that messaging 'needs to emphasise and explain the duty to protect others' and should 'be framed positively in terms of protecting oneself and the community, and increase confidence that they will be effective'. So the SAGE subgroup was not arguing that facts should be trumped up, but that people were taking false comfort from the fact that COVID-19 was more lethal among the elderly and vulnerable and therefore they needn't change *their own* behaviour. To contain the virus and protect the NHS from being overwhelmed, it would be necessary not just for the vulnerable but for *everyone* to change their behaviour because, as has been understood through centuries of plague-control measures, some diseases can spread by ordinary social interaction. The paper also considered coercion as an option and recommended that 'consideration . . . be given to enacting legislation . . . to compel key social distancing measures' but warned that 'data from Italy and South Korea suggest that for aggressive protective measures to be effective, special attention should be devoted to those population groups that are more at risk'.

In other words, the SAGE paper was recommending more or less what Lord Sumption proposed: people should be given a true appreciation of the risks to themselves and others so they could be empowered to make their own decisions, and any measures involving coercion should be focused particularly on those most at risk. What in fact happened the day after the date of the SAGE paper was the institution of a national lockdown, compelling everyone to behave the same, regardless of risk. But when the government attempted, during the summer and autumn of 2020, to vary measures according to areas so that they could be more precisely targeted, that policy brought its own problems of plummeting public understanding of the rules and an increasing sense (whether or not accurate) that some parts of the country, such as the North, were being unfairly singled out. Counterintuitively, more targeted measures may have made people feel less empowered to make their own decisions.

What is also clear, admittedly in retrospect, is that in late November 2020 Sumption and others were mistaken about the *danger* – and as wrong to underplay it then as they had been in March 2020. As soon as the November lockdown ended the case rates rapidly climbed, shortly followed by the death rates, which by mid-December were over 500 per day, peaking in mid-January at over 1,000 per day, by far the highest rate of the pandemic. In the three months from 20 November, 66,794 people would die in the UK after testing positive for COVID-19, not far off a third of the total deaths for the entire pandemic.[32] Over 65,000 deaths *in three months*. Over 65,000 lives ended prematurely, families decimated, many more left without parents or grandparents. If ever there was a case for a few months of self-sacrifice, of 'lending our liberty', then surely this was it.

The right which lockdown sceptics always seemed to forget, or downplay, is the very first on the list in the Human Rights Act: the right to life. The state must do all it reasonably can to protect the rights of those it has responsibility over. And what about responsibilities? Those who oppose or are sceptical about human rights often raise the (largely imagined) idea that human rights pay no regard to the responsibilities we have towards others. But inherent in the idea that we give our state the power to decide when certain liberties must give way to others is the acceptance that we cannot always do as we feel, or even pursue simply what is best for us as individuals. Our individual rights must sometimes give way to the good of the collective. That this can create unfairness, or even the brute force of utilitarianism (the greatest good for the greatest number), is hardly a revelation – it has been a preoccupation of moral philosophers for centuries. To reiterate: the only proven methods to prevent the spread of COVID-19 without a vaccine (which was by this stage tantalisingly close) were quarantine (supported by test and trace), self-isolation and social distancing. Whether that should be done by coercion or persuasion, or a mix of both, how much the government should control without scrutiny, and *which* freedoms should give way were fundamentally important questions, but also fundamentally different questions to whether social distancing was necessary at all.

They are questions which Lord Sumption pointedly raised,

and, looking back now, I agree with much of his critique. But if you start from the premise that some measures are necessary, the questions of how hard, and how soon, are also hugely important, but they were generally avoided by those who rejected the idea of any restrictions. These are questions which epidemiologists, political scientists and the COVID-19 public inquiry will wrestle with for years to come. My guess is that they will conclude the government erred by assuming in September it could avoid lockdown, or could do a half-hearted lockdown, and that – almost paradoxically – an earlier and sharper lockdown would have impacted on rights less in the medium term, as well as saving tens of thousands of lives.

To Christmas or not to Christmas

On 2 December 2020, the second lockdown ended and the three tiers returned, this time in a single 76-page mammoth regulation.[33] Almost the whole of England would go into the two highest tiers, both of which included significant restrictions on gatherings but no stay-at-home order. Only 1 per cent of the population would go into Tier 1 – 700,000 people compared to the 23.5 million who were in Tier 1 before the November lockdown. There was a new exception for 'Linked Christmas Households', the idea being to carve out five days from 23 to 27 December when people would have a break from gathering restrictions and could make up their own minds whether to put themselves and their friends and relatives at risk from COVID-19. It would essentially be a pause to restrictions, a bit like the football match that warring troops played against each other during the 1914 'Christmas truce'. But it turned out that the virus was not interested in truces.

Two important things happened in early December which

showed how entrenched the Emergency State had become. The first was that Parliament briefly sparked to life, but to little effect, and the second was that the courts began to review the legality of the coronavirus regulations.

The new 'All Tiers' regulations were to be debated, and voted in, on 1 December, the day before they came into force. For the first time, the Labour Party told its MPs to abstain on, rather than support, COVID-19 regulations. It was reported that Keir Starmer said to his MPs that he did not believe Labour should directly oppose the measures, because of the need to keep control of the virus, but that, by abstaining, the party could signal that the financial support for hospitality businesses was inadequate. The Liberal Democrats refused to support the new tiers, calling them 'arbitrary, confused and chaotic'. The government, for its part, accused the opposition of 'playing politics'.[34] But by that logic so were some of its own MPs, with 55 Conservative MPs opposing the measures in the final vote, which otherwise easily passed, with 291 for (all Conservative) and 78 against.

The rebellion had been stoked by the newly formed Covid Recovery Group (CRG), made up of Conservative backbenchers who said the restrictions were 'authoritarianism at work'. Graham Brady, the influential MP for Sale and Altrincham West, a constituency which was to be placed into the strictest tier, said the new system 'interfered in people's private and personal lives in a way which is unacceptable'.[35] Steve Baker, the CRG's Deputy Chair, said the tiers were 'truly appalling' and, notably using the language of human rights, questioned whether they were 'necessary and proportionate'. Baker would also become an influential voice against restrictions. The CRG questioned why most of the country was emerging from a lockdown that had been sold to them on the basis it would only be for four weeks, only to be plunged into harsh restrictions. The reality was that the lockdown had caused the numbers to plateau, but they immediately began to climb after it ended. This was, ultimately, not a real Parliamentary rebellion but a shot across the Prime Minister's bows. Indeed, the threat from the libertarian right of the Conservative Party, now formally coalesced into the CRG, appears to have worried the Prime Minister far more than the risk of MPs voting down the restrictions, and may have been the cause of the half-heartedness of the measures in autumn 2020.

The courts keep out of it

As if inspired by Parliament's brief awakening, the courts began from early December to consider the COVID-19 measures in earnest. The first major case relating to the pandemic was brought by Simon Dolan, a wealthy British businessman who lived in Monaco but owned a business in Britain and visited the country to see family and friends. In May 2020 he had set up the Keep Britain Free group to campaign against lockdowns and to 'ensure that our freedoms and our right to our freedoms as people of a Democratic country, are NON NEGOTIABLE'.[36] With two others claimants, Dolan launched a judicial review (a legal claim to challenge the lawfulness of a public authority's decision) of the March 2020 lockdown regulations. They alleged that the lockdown regulations went further than the Public Health Act allowed, that they breached various public law principles and that they violated human rights.[37]

The Court of Appeal, led by the Lord Chief Justice, Lord Burnett, dismissed the claim in its entirety.[38] The court said the Health Secretary had power under the Public Health Act to make even the vastly restrictive lockdown regulations. This was because the 'purpose of the new regime introduced in 2008 was to cater for the possibility of a much greater public health response which might be needed in order to deal with an epidemic', and this was 'precisely in order to meet a modern epidemic such as that caused by SARS in the early part of this century'. I am dubious that anyone in Parliament had national lockdowns in mind in 2008 – even the brief reference in debates to the measures during the SARS epidemic in Hong Kong can only have been references to the quarantining of small parts of a city, not a whole city, let alone an entire nation. I am therefore not convinced that Parliament was really giving power to the Secretary of State to quarantine an entire national population, by secondary legislation, with the option of not consulting Parliament for four weeks.

It is clear from the other parts of the judgment that the court would give the government a wide discretion to make the almost impossibly difficult decisions necessary to address the COVID-19 pandemic. This is an area, the court said, 'in which the Secretary of State had to make difficult judgements about medical and scientific issues and did so after taking advice from relevant experts'. It quoted a previous judgment of Lord Bingham, saying that 'on public health issues which require the evaluation of complex scientific evidence, the national court may and should be slow to interfere with a decision which a responsible decision-maker has reached after consultation with its expert advisers'. There were 'powerfully expressed conflicting views about many of the measures taken by the Government and how various balances should be struck', but this was 'quintessentially a matter of political judgement for the Government, which is accountable to Parliament, and is not suited to determination by the courts'. The lockdown did not breach the rights to private and family life because, although it obviously interfered with those rights, a 'wide margin of judgement must be afforded to the Government and to Parliament' on 'well-established grounds both of democratic accountability and institutional competence'. On the right to protest, since a person could only commit a criminal offence if they did not have a 'reasonable excuse' (the language of the regulations), this could include exercising the right to protest. This finding would become important in a later case about the right to protest.

When I first read the *Dolan* judgment I felt that the Court of Appeal may have had its *Liversidge v Anderson* moment, being, as Lord Atkin had said in that case, 'more executive-minded than the executive'. The timing for the claimants was terrible – at the beginning of December 2020, case rates were still high and the country was about to emerge tentatively from a national lockdown, a kind of pressure that I imagine made it psychologically more difficult for judges to act in a way which might be interpreted as undermining the government's efforts to deal with a deadly emergency. I also suspect that it will not have gone unnoticed to the court, even if subconsciously, that the claim was brought by a high-profile anti-lockdown campaigner.

The court may have got it right on the human rights arguments. If the only tool you have is a hammer, it is tempting to treat everything as if it were a nail. And for human rights lawyers, it is tempting to treat every problem as if it is one which can be solved by a court applying human rights principles. There were reasonable human rights arguments for lockdowns, based on the state's duty to protect life and the health of the population; and reasonable human rights arguments against, citing the enormous collateral damage to family lives, religious observance, protest, mental health and education. Ultimately, the judges approached the case as not being about *what* the right approach was but *who* was to make the big calls. There is a powerful argument for the answer being Parliament, not the courts, because in times of emergency that is where the buck stops. But this is *not* to say that the courts should be excluded altogether from scrutiny of the many decisions made by public authorities during an emergency which gravely impact on rights.

My main concern about the Dolan case is that the court did not even permit a full hearing (which would have been triggered if the judges had concluded the case was 'arguable'), where the government would have been forced to present the evidence which supported its decisions – not just the decision to lock down, but also which activities to permit and which to prohibit. The court's default position, that huge social policy calls are a matter for Parliaments not courts, can be justified in times of calm, when government decisions are subject to proper democratic oversight. But things are different in the Emergency State. Parliament had all but surrendered its usual role of holding government to account. If the court had allowed a full hearing, with the government being forced to justify its actions with evidence, and the claimants being able to demand to see the working behind the government's opaque decision-making, this could have mitigated some of the democratic failings of the COVID-19 period. It would, at the least, have given the public a valuable insight into the reasoning behind decisions – made by a tiny committee of MPs without publishing minutes. In the Emergency State, institutions need to step up or risk being seen as complicit. Could it really be the case that the most extreme intrusion in human rights for eight decades was not worth a full hearing by the High Court?

It is notable that there has been no decision of the European Court of Human Rights – the ultimate arbiter of European human rights law – which has criticised lockdowns. This may change in years to come, as courts analyse decisions at more distance from the acute trauma of a public health emergency. But, for now, I believe the court in Simon Dolan's case was too risk-averse – though, I should also say that the court's approach reflects my own reticence during the pandemic to use human rights arguments to contest lockdown generally, despite the very regular cries of 'shame' aimed at me from lockdown sceptics, and despite Lord Sumption, who said that human rights defenders had been 'extraordinarily silent' over lockdown.[39] The difference, though, between the court and me is that the court had the power to demand that the government justify its decisions from a human rights perspective, and could have then considered those arguments in detail. The result may, ultimately, have been the same, but the process would have been hugely valuable.

On whether the regulations were within the powers granted by the Public Health Act, I think the court also dismissed this argument too easily. It may be correct to leave big policy calls involving complex scientific and political considerations to the government, but if the justification for that is 'democratic accountability', then the democratic mechanism being used must be rock solid. The 2008 changes to the Public Health Act were brought in before the idea of the mass quarantine of individuals was being considered, or had been experienced, by anyone in Parliament. And since the regulations themselves were passed without prior Parliamentary scrutiny, the democratic basis for the restrictions looks shaky too.

The Dolan case was by no means the last word from the courts, but it remains probably the most important, as it shut down any possible *general* challenge to lockdown laws.

Christmas is cancelled, and New Year too

December 2020 was dominated by debate over whether Christmas gatherings would be cancelled. And as the holiday approached, and case and death rates soared, the government increased restrictions. On 15 December, the Prime Minister said he did not want to ban or cancel Christmas, as that would be 'inhuman'.[40] London was placed into Tier 3, the highest tier, the following day.[41] Then, on 20 December, a fourth tier arrived. This was in effect a full lockdown, as it included a stay-at-home order.[42] Tier 4 included London and much of the South and East of England. At least the government could no longer be accused of picking on the North. Overnight stays away from home were banned and the guidance was clear that we 'should not enter or leave Tier 4 areas'. For the first time, there truly was a local lockdown. Christmas gatherings were not permitted in Tier 4 areas at all, and in the lower tiers they were reduced from five days to one.

On 6 January 2021, the rest of England was placed into Tier 4, marking the beginning of the third – and, to date, final – national lockdown.[43] For the first time since June 2020, schools and universities were largely shut. Religious services, meanwhile, remained open with social distancing and a prohibition on mingling (from my own perspective, as a regular synagogue attendee, this was welcome, although the removal of the traditional 'kiddush', or light meal, at the service's conclusion seemed particularly harsh). While it was welcome that religious services could go ahead, respecting the right to manifest one's religion and also providing comfort for many during a dark period, it was odd that it was legal to have a crowd of a hundred inside a church but not ten people outdoors protesting, or indeed watching sports. This seemed an obvious and unjustified skewing of priorities, which no doubt reflected the concerns of the tiny group of people responsible for the regulations, rather than any logical assessment of risk.

The ever-changing rules were so confusing that I started releasing YouTube videos explaining them.[44] I even recorded a video with Dr Xand van Tulleken, presenter of my daughter's favourite TV programme, *Operation Ouch!*, who helped explain how to mitigate the risks from Christmas gatherings. I was increasingly being called on by the media to help people understand the rules – and looking back, given how regularly they changed, were rebranded and reimagined, it is hardly surprising.

Never in my wildest imaginings did I expect to find myself on *Good Morning Britain* on 11 January 2021, being asked by Piers Morgan whether it was legal to sit on a park bench. What hope did anyone who was not obsessively following the regulations have of understanding them?

The even thinner blue line

I knew several police officers followed me on Twitter, as I was regularly receiving messages saying that they were relying on my feed to find out about the new criminal laws and what they meant. On 10 January, as the third national lockdown began, I asked on Twitter for serving officers to message me about how things were going from their perspective. I received around twenty responses.[45]

There were some clear themes. First, plenty of embarrassment over what officers saw as 'over enforcement' of the regulations. One Metropolitan Police officer was 'ashamed and embarrassed' about how some of the 'more Northern Constabularies' had behaved. Another said they were 'relieved to have avoided some of the embarrassments seen by neighbouring forces' over-zealous targeting of walkers etc'. The 'targeting of walkers' and 'over-zealous' Northern constabularies references were to a notorious incident when Derbyshire police gave £200 Fixed Penalty Notices to two walkers who had driven five miles for a walk around a reservoir. The police initially said that driving for exercise was 'not in the spirit of the lockdown'. I made the point that police were not Ghostbusters and should not be enforcing the 'spirit' of anything, just the letter of the law. The FPNs were withdrawn after a public outcry. It was therefore no surprise that one police officer told me that they 'cringe' at 'cops . . . attempting to enforce guidance not law'. Not all police were 'officiously chasing joggers', said another, recognising that the Covid restrictions are 'the biggest infringement of human rights ever' and the police 'need public support, now and in the future'. That said, an officer in a Northern force told me not to believe the *Daily Mail* 'All Police are Bullies' story and that they could tell me '100%' that 'enforcement of COVID [regulations] is the absolute last resort' and only for 'absolute idiots' who think they are 'above the law'.

A second theme was that the regulations were very difficult to enforce. One exasperated officer said:

> There has often been a gap between what the UK govt thinks the police can do (enforce any law, immediately, against any proportion of the population) and what is operationally possible/desirable. That gap has led to confused strategy . . . On numerous occasions, have read news articles about legislation I'm expected to enforce 24-48hrs before any official communication comes out about the *existence* of new offences (or the cessation of offences) never mind what the strategy is going to be.

It is 'very frustrating', said another officer, 'that the guidance does not reflect the law' and that the regulations were 'not clear on key areas (protests for example) and the onus is on the police forces to decide what is permissible'. When the Chair of the Police Federation gave evidence to the Joint Committee on Human Rights, he said that he thought nine out of ten officers felt the regulations were not clear.[46] The exasperation was shared by others. One officer told me that the rules were 'a farce and pretty much unenforceable'. Those who willingly breach the guidelines 'we can't stop', whereas the ones who breach them by mistake 'are the ones we end up arguing with'. Finally, 'we're people too . . . [the job of police] is not as bad as hospitals but we're tired, we're angry and we're scared, and it feels like everyone hates us'.

Low morale was a consistent theme – particularly as it was

not always clear why enforcement was necessary for low-level breaches. 'Although the overall risk to public safety . . . is high', one officer said, 'the average breach the police are called to is low risk, in the wider scheme of things . . . [t]hat combination – collective high risk, individual low risk, is difficult to police well.' By January 2021, another reported, they were surprised at how many calls they got from 'neighbour reporting on neighbour', a worrying sign that the social cohesion which was just as important as the enforcement of regulations for getting through the pandemic was being eroded.

Contrary to the occasional press report of overreach, a number of officers who contacted me thought that the UK's policing of the lockdown had been light touch. This was a reflection of the policing culture we have here, which is 'to be celebrated' but also 'possibly not well suited to pandemic management'. Police 'could be setting up road blocks, questioning everyone seen on the streets as to their reasonable excuse', but this did not fit with the '4Es' strategy, which was aimed at letting 'people manage the risk themselves'. This was in contrast to how 'much more strict police in other European countries' such as France or Italy were, where policing legitimacy is lower 'but they almost certainly have stopped more COVID than us'.

This was not just an impression. Enforcement of coronavirus restrictions in some major European states was a lot stricter than in the UK. In England and Wales, 118,978 FPNs were issued between 27 March 2020 and 27 February 2022.[47] That amounts to around one for every 500 people. By contrast, in France, over 760,000 fines were issued – about one fine for every eighty people – and 12.6 million police checks undertaken in the first month of the 2020 lockdown.[48] In Spain, over a million fines were given out during the three-month state of emergency which began in March 2020,[49] around one for every forty-three people, although these ultimately had to be paid back after the initial state of emergency was struck down by the Constitutional Court.[50] In Italy, 568,356 fines were handed out from March 2020 to November 2021, around one fine for every 105 people.[51] So in France, Spain and Italy, proportionately between five and ten times more fines were given out by law enforcement.

An important question for post-pandemic Britain is whether the police were indeed given an impossible task, as I had suggested by April 2020, or if they were given a difficult job and did their muddled best. And perhaps whether the police were not the right public authority to enforce COVID-19 rules and that this task should have been given to public health officers supported by the police, as suggested by one of the officers who contacted me. This will be a matter that the COVID-19 public inquiry will consider, and it should do so with reference to international comparators, bearing in mind varying policing cultures and different national attitudes towards the harsh, temporary social distancing rules which were imposed during the pandemic. Whatever the answer, I have no doubt that enforcing the COVID-19 laws was one of the most challenging, and at times demoralising, tasks the police have ever been given.

The darkest month

In early January 2021, an opinion piece in the *British Medical Journal* argued that the term 'pandemic fatigue' – behavioural fatigue associated with long-term Covid restrictions – had been wrongly cited as a reason for delaying new rules and loosening restrictions. However, levels of adherence to strict regulations remained 'extremely high', at over 90 per cent, even though many suffered both financially and psychologically. The exception was self-isolation rules, where adherence was estimated to be around 18 per cent. The authors proposed that international comparisons suggested this was caused by a failure of government support for those who were isolating. They concluded that instead of stories about fatigue, the headlines 'should highlight the remarkable and enduring resilience of the great majority of the population – including those who have been most subject to blame such as students and young people in general – even in the absence of adequate support and guidance from government'. Moreover, 'in many ways the narratives of blame serve to project the real frailties of government policy onto the imagined frailties of public psychology'.[52]

But despite the *BMJ*'s efforts, the narrative of 'covidiots' dominated a very dark January. The death rates were by far the highest of the pandemic, with a horrifying high of 1,820 reported on 20 January 2021 alone, driven by the new B.1.1.7 variant. In January 2021, 30,472 people in the UK died after receiving a positive diagnosis of COVID-19.[53] The government seemed keen to blame people partying while others were locked down, with the Home Secretary, Priti Patel, announcing a new £800 FPN for people attending indoor gatherings of over fifteen people without a reasonable excuse. It is notable that, at this time, SAGE's Environmental Modelling Group was recommending against 'crackdowns', saying instead that the government should suggest 'positive solutions, maintain social cohesion and support, and promote a shared sense of responsibility for infection control'. Fear-inducing messages, it warned, 'should be avoided'.[54]

The courts were now considering COVID-19 cases more regularly and I was spending a lot of time advising clients on a huge range of matters relating to the regulations. One issue arose at Napier Barracks in Kent, used to house asylum seekers since September 2020. The barracks were squalid and unsanitary, with a fire leading to limited electricity and hot water. Living conditions were so cramped – fourteen men sharing a room – that there was no prospect for any kind of quarantine or isolation. After a predictable COVID-19 outbreak, all residents were told they could not leave the barracks under any circumstances – even though this was not a detention centre and the self-isolation rules (if they applied) permitted people to leave for various essential reasons including to avoid the risk of harm. I assisted in applying for urgent High Court orders, essentially test cases, for the Home Office to transfer a number of the residents to safer accommodation. These were granted.[55] Later, the High Court would rule that housing vulnerable asylum seekers, who were not supposed to be detained, in overcrowded, noisy and inadequate accommodation was unlawful.[56] The conditions placed them at a high risk of contracting COVID-19. The court also ruled that the residents were falsely imprisoned because of a notice issued in mid-January which stated that they were 'not to leave the site under any circumstance' and that 'if you have been found to disregard this advice, the Police may issue you with a Fixed Penalty Notice or you may be arrested'. The notice had no legal foundation.

The Napier Barracks case was about how the Home Office was treating asylum seekers, but it also reflected some wider themes. The COVID-19 laws were creating nationwide confusion, including among those most obliged to understand them – ministers, the police and the Home Office. A similar situation had arisen in November 2020 when, without warning students, the University of Manchester erected fences around halls of residence. Students were only able to leave through a single guarded exit. This led to hundreds of them angrily protesting what they called 'HMP Fallowfield' and ripping down some of the fences. The university ultimately apologised for a misguided attempt to quarantine students.[57] Through cases which were referred to me, I saw these themes again and again: but if these egregious cases happened to be referred to me, how many *more* were occurring, unseen and unheard? How many injustices being caused by misunderstandings, or even exploitation, of these ever-changing, oppressive laws? On the other hand, some injustices *were* being exposed: the Emergency State had not entirely neutered the courts.

Forgetting the Human Rights Act

The police continued to misunderstand their duties under the Human Rights Act. From the cases of a number of clients I was advising who were attempting to protest, it was obvious that the police were acting as if protests were banned completely, even though the January lockdown regulations said nothing at all about banning them. Absurdly, in late January 2021, police in North London threatened two men with arrest for protesting outside a Volkswagen garage against the car company's factory in the Xinjiang region of China, where millions of Uighur Muslims are imprisoned in concentration camps.[58] The two men had been protesting weekly for two years, including at the Chinese Embassy, but were suddenly told by the police this was no longer permitted.[59] Protest was being policed as if it was illegal, ignoring the police's duty under the Human Rights Act; little wonder, since the College of Police and NPCC guidance failed to mention the rights to free speech and protest.[60]

I was encountering other similar examples, and not just involving protesters. On 26 January, the police gave FPNs to Mayor of London candidate Brian Rose for campaigning on the city's streets. A video was released of the police telling Rose that political campaigning did not follow the 'essence' of the lockdown.[61] This was oppressive and, I strongly suspect, unlawful behaviour. The position in law should have been simple. The

Human Rights Act is primary legislation, an act of Parliament, which grants people rights but also imposes clear legal duties on public authorities, including the police, not to act in a way which is incompatible with those rights.[62] The coronavirus regulations were secondary legislation and also vague – both the stay-at-home and gatherings restrictions were subject to 'reasonable excuses'. There was a list of potential reasonable excuses but it was non-exhaustive, meaning there were always potential reasonable excuses which were not listed. And the Court of Appeal had made clear in Simon Dolan's case that one reasonable excuse would be that an individual was exercising their human rights, for example to protest. The police had no power to do anything under the regulations unless they believed an offence was being committed – and there could be no offence if someone was exercising their human rights in a proportionate way. The simple point is that where there was ambiguity, and fundamental rights were at stake, the coronavirus regulations should always have given way to the Human Rights Act, *especially* where they had not explicitly banned activities like protest and political campaigning.

Hotel quarantine checks in

One of the odd aspects of the government's COVID-19 strategy was that, from a proportionality perspective, it seemed to be happening back to front. Ordinarily, you would expect the state to begin by quarantining those most likely to be infected and isolating those who are infected. If that does not work, you can cast the quarantine net wider. But the UK government did the opposite. It began, in March 2020, with the quarantining of the entire population, regardless of the likelihood of infection. It was not until six months later that it became a legal requirement to isolate if you were infected, or to quarantine after close contact with someone who was infected – a far more targeted use of the criminal law. And it was not until five months after that that there was mandatory isolation for people who came to England from places where COVID-19 rates or variants were a particular problem.

By early 2021, however belatedly, the government was becoming concerned about new COVID-19 variants arriving on our shores from abroad and decided that it would follow some other countries' approach – notably Australia – by forcing travellers to quarantine in hotel rooms. As had become traditional by then, this major policy was not formally announced but leaked to the *Daily Telegraph*, the newspaper in which the Prime Minister had a column until 2019.[63] The policy was to introduce a legal requirement for anyone arriving from a country on the 'red list' to buy a 'managed self-isolation package', which would include a hotel room booking, transport, and a testing package.[64] The package would cost £1,750 per adult and between £325 and £650 for each child, with an option to pay in instalments if travellers were facing 'significant financial hardship'. Once you arrived at your hotel, you would be confined to a room for at least ten clear days (but potentially longer if you tested positive for COVID-19). There were very limited reasons you could leave your hotel room: essentially for emergencies only, or for exercise, but only if permitted by the hotel staff. The hotel quarantine regulations were published on Friday 12 February and came into force on Monday 15. Shockingly, even by the standards of the COVID-19 Emergency State, the scheme that effectively detained hundreds of thousands of travellers – including thousands of children – was not approved by Parliament in advance and indeed was not debated until five weeks later, on 22 March.[65]

But the lack of Parliamentary scrutiny was just one issue. The hotel quarantine system itself was very troubling and seemed to have escaped any serious and detailed consideration of its implications. The word 'hotel' implied cushy conditions for travellers. They were not. People were confined not to a *hotel* for ten days but to their *room*, which generally had windows that were sealed shut. G4S security guards were often stationed in the corridor outside to prevent people leaving their rooms. Access to common parts of the hotel was banned except for very limited periods of exercise, usually fifteen minutes per day in the hotel car park. Food was delivered three times a day but was often late, of poor quality or did not allow for special dietary requirements.[66] In June 2021, four women told the BBC that they had been sexually harassed by G4S guards while in hotel quarantine.[67] One guard mimed having sex when he and one of the women were alone in a lift; then, on another day, he told her his testicles were burning. Another stepped into a woman's room asking for a hug while delivering an Amazon package. A third woman was propositioned by a guard, after which he followed her during exercise and stationed himself outside her room when she returned. Other women said that guards had been intimidating or abusive.

I started to receive phone calls about people stuck in the quarantine system whose presence there was entirely inappropriate, usually because they had a serious medical condition. There was a sensible-sounding medical exception in the regulations, if you could show that a person was vulnerable as a result of a severe health condition or would not receive appropriate support during the hotel quarantine or their condition would be likely to be severely detrimentally impacted. But the reality was that applications for the exemption, presented with all the supporting evidence, hit the brick wall of Department of Health officials; particularly in the first weeks of hotel quarantine, government officials seemed to be taking a 'refuse everyone' approach. Time and again I saw the copied and pasted refusal: 'the bar for exemption is incredibly high and we have to remain robust and consistent in our approach'. The team was 'confident' that the individual could be kept safely in hotel quarantine – but did not explain how. This did not fill me or my clients with confidence.

One example illustrates the reality: my client, a severely disabled child, was refused an exemption despite providing evidence of his severe and complex needs. The initial application was refused without reasoning. The family were then told that the family room they had requested was no longer available – this meant the child was in a separate room, and every time his parents left their room to check on him they were questioned by security guards. No food was provided when they arrived. The parents submitted evidence from the child's treating psychologist explaining why his particular needs could not be met in hotel quarantine, and that it would likely lead to a severe deterioration. Meanwhile, the harsh conditions began to have the predicted effect on the child's condition. I and the other lawyers I was working with met with the increasingly distressed family by Zoom and decided, given the urgency, that we needed to take the issue to the High Court.[68] Following a number of hearings over the weekend, the duty judge ruled that the child had reasonable prospects of showing that the Department of Health's decision was unlawful and gave the government until 12 p.m. the next day to obtain its own expert evidence. On Monday morning, minutes before the final hearing, the government agreed the family could complete their quarantine at home – having by now spent a week in the hotel. In a radio interview afterwards, my client's father spoke of the extreme stress of the experience, which had 'had an immediate and detrimental impact' on his son.[69]

In another case, I acted for Zaina Erhaim, an award-winning

Syrian journalist and refugee whose multiple requests for an exemption were left unanswered by the Health Secretary.[70] While working for the BBC in Syria, Erhaim was kidnapped by militias working for the Assad regime and held prisoner in a room for two days, leaving her with post-traumatic stress disorder, predictably triggered after she was confined in a guarded hotel room. She was eventually released once we had made legal submissions to the Health Secretary, but the damage was done. Afterwards, Erhaim said that she had expected brutality and intimidation in Syria, but in hotel quarantine she was 'yet again treated like a criminal without doing any crime . . . imprisoned in a hotel room with guards', and, unlike when she was kidnapped in Syria, 'this time I had my daughter with me, which made everything much harder'.

I also worked on judicial review challenges to the hotel quarantine system.[71] One succeeded and one did not. The first was a challenge to the policy that meant *everyone* who came through hotel quarantine had to pay the fee, which, for a family, would be thousands of pounds, regardless of means or circumstances. Other than the option to pay in instalments, there was no distinction made between a millionaire who had gone on a skiing holiday and a broke pensioner who had travelled abroad for a funeral. After receiving the pre-action letter, the government conceded that there needed to be allowance made for people suffering from 'severe financial hardship' who were travelling for essential reasons. A new policy was released a few months later.[72]

A second systemic challenge failed. This was a harder one, as if we had succeeded it could have unravelled the whole system, or at least prevented the quarantine of double-vaccinated travellers. We said that the hotel quarantine breached the right to liberty, protected by Article 5 of the European Convention on Human Rights. But to show a breach of the right to liberty you first have to prove that a person is detained, and the High Court had already decided, in a different case, that being confined to a guarded room with no exercise except with permission, no opening windows, and food delivered to the door, did not amount to detention. The judge in our case was reticent not to follow that previous decision but concluded that, even if there was a detention, there was no realistic prospect of a court concluding that the hotel quarantine scheme was disproportionate. Evaluative policy questions were 'matters entrusted to government, with the scrutiny of Parliament and public scrutiny'.[73] This was the same message as in the Dolan case, and indeed in all of the legal challenges to the coronavirus regulations: a reluctance by the courts to interfere with controversial COVID-19 policies. I am sure it did not help that the hearing was held at the height of the Omicron outbreak in December 2021. Yet the troubling aspect was that the court refused even to have a full hearing, with evidence, which would have forced the government to fully justify its policy. At a bare minimum, a system which amounted to detention for thousands of adults and children should receive proper scrutiny. Parliament had barely touched the issue – and I knew from my work how many injustices were happening in these private-security-guarded hotels.

As I said about the Dolan case, it is tempting for human rights lawyers to assume that all issues can be resolved by the courts. Some cannot, and are ultimately for democratically elected governments. But when *nobody* is looking, surely somebody needs to take responsibility. As of August 2021, approximately sixty people out of tens of thousands who went through the hotel quarantine system had been granted medical exemptions.[74] By the time hotel quarantine ended on 15 December 2021,[75] over 210,000 people – including, I assume, many thousands of children – had been confined.[76] One day, the full story will be told.

8. Step by Step

1 February 2021 to 18 March 2022
Cases: 16,312,077
Deaths: 55,457
Cumulative deaths: 165,942

From 31 December 2019 to January 2021, events happened at an almost unbearable speed and intensity. In the UK, over 100,000 had died 'before their time', as the Prime Minister had warned they would back in March 2020, though I doubt he imagined it would be so many. He himself had almost died. Meanwhile, his government had lurched from national lockdown, to local lockdowns, to tiers, to two more national lockdowns, backed by ever more complex rules and ever less respect for democratic process. But just as it seemed that the frenetic cycle would never end, the COVID-19 vaccine arrived. The imposition of lockdowns had been justified by the government in part as a stopgap solution while the vaccine was being developed. Now it was here, would the cycle of COVID-19 waves, and lockdowns to suppress them, end? Was 'freedom day' imminent?

Daily deaths were at the highest point in the pandemic, but in January 2021 case rates declined. By mid-February, deaths were declining too, though still at over 500 per day. Thankfully, the vaccination programme, initiated in December 2020, was up and running. Hundreds of thousands of people per day were, as Matt Hancock kept saying, 'injecting hope' into their arms and, on 22 February, the government set out its plan for 'reopening'. Since levels of infection were broadly similar across England, the Prime Minister said, the measures would change at the same time, in a series of 'Steps'. Schools would open on 8 March, shops no earlier than 12 April, then indoor pubs and restaurants along with sports stadia no earlier than 21 June, when all the remaining restrictions would be removed. This slow emergence from restrictions would allow the vaccination programme, in another Hancockism, to 'ramp up'.[1]

Vaccine passports and Godwin's Law

As part of the gradual plan to emerge from lockdown, the government also said that it was considering bringing in 'Covid certificates', also known as vaccine passports, which would be necessary to access social activities such as concerts, or even supermarkets, mirroring the 'Green Pass' system which had been implemented in Israel, the first country to institute mass vaccination. But it was not until 13 December 2021 that the UK introduced COVID passes, as the Omicron variant caused case numbers to soar.[2] By the time the idea of COVID passes was suggested (a more accurate name than vaccine passports as proposals always included *both* vaccination and recent infection), the anti-vaccine and anti-lockdown movement had become louder and more extreme, if not particularly effective at shifting public opinion in the UK. The movement's extremism was symbolised by the regular likening of COVID passes to the yellow Star of David which Jewish people were made to wear during the Holocaust. In Germany (of all places), anti-lockdown protesters took to wearing a version of the yellow star with the word 'Jude' (Jew) replaced by 'ungeimpft' (unvaccinated), and in the UK the stars were branded with the word 'COVID'.[3] COVID passes may have been controversial, but they could be justified. Jews, however, were made to wear Stars of David so they could be singled out for discrimination, dehumanisation and ultimately mass murder. The comparison was grotesque. 'Nuremberg Code' would often trend on Twitter in this period as some argued, with similar levels of offensiveness, that COVID-19 vaccinations were analogous to the inhumane experimentation undertaken by Nazi doctors on human subjects.[4]

Godwin's Law is the internet adage that, as an online discussion gets longer, the probability of a comparison to the Nazis or Adolf Hitler increases, regardless of the subject. But the Nazi comparison to COVID-19 measures was particularly common. I think this was due to a combination of two factors. First, severe restrictions on freedoms were being instigated by governments worldwide, and after a year were stubbornly persisting – even increasing – despite the promised silver bullet of vaccinations. Any severe restrictions on civil liberties will inevitably lead to comparisons with nondemocratic or totalitarian regimes, and in the West there is no more resonant a comparator than Hitler's Nazis. The second reason was the shift towards individualised rights that COVID passes represented compared to the blunt approach represented by lockdowns. As the pandemic wore on, one fundamental fact had changed: whereas in March 2020 almost nobody was protected from COVID-19, either by antibodies generated by previous infection or by a vaccine, in March 2021 millions of people were, and it was possible to distinguish the people who were less at risk of catching, and therefore transmitting,[5] COVID-19. It is harder to justify an indiscriminate lockdown when you have a simple way to distinguish those who are at less risk of being infected with COVID-19. But discrimination comes with its own problems, as had been demonstrated by the experiment during the summer and autumn with local lockdowns. The sense of 'all in this together' is replaced by what appears to be a hierarchy, or a system based partly on arbitrary factors. From the perspective of a person who has decided not to take the vaccine – perhaps not because they are a conspiracy theorist who believes Bill Gates is using vaccinations for mind control,[6] but due to fears about taking relatively new vaccinations – they may feel that they are being discriminated against because of a legitimate choice.

I view COVID passes as another agonising policy question which, from a human rights perspective, has no straightforward answer.[7] Valid concerns about COVID passes include the fact that they potentially create a two-tier society, because they can exclude from social activities those who cannot or will not get vaccinated. They would be the thin end of a wedge opening the door to digital identity cards, giving public authorities such as the police access to biometric and health data. Possible advantages were that rather than imposing indiscriminate lockdowns, states could use COVID passes to better calibrate movement and gathering restrictions so that risks posed by particular individuals could be taken into account, even at the 'micro' level, such as when entering venues such as pubs. This had been made possible by the advent of mass testing, vaccination and – indeed – mass infection, none of which had happened before the first lockdown was imposed. Lockdowns, which severely curtail a vast range of rights, should always be the *last resort* – but in order to make that phrase mean something, you have to properly engage with what other, potentially unpalatable, policies you can resort to. COVID passes might have been the worst option available apart from all the others that had been tried. The counter-argument would be that to accept lockdowns as inevitable *without* COVID passes would be to look through the wrong end of the telescope: the presumption should always be against mass restrictions, and we risked sleepwalking into accepting limits on our freedoms which until recently would have been inconceivable, but could now be justified by the mantra of 'well, at least it's better than a lockdown'. Because, some might say, *anything* is better than lockdown.

Ultimately, what you think about COVID passes probably depends on whether you agree that mass enforced social distancing was ever justified. If you do not, then you cannot reasonably accept another unattractive policy option is justified because the alternative is worse. You would argue that neither is justified and therefore neither should be used. My conclusion at the time was essentially a fudge: there are human rights arguments for and against COVID passes. And the underlying truth was that COVID-19 had at that time killed over 100,000 people in the UK, and without some kind of social distancing measures, in combination with the vaccination and testing programmes, it was likely to infect and kill many more. COVID passes may or may not be the right policy, but it seemed a reasonable one to explore. In that context, the comparison to Nazi Germany – a murderous regime built on a racial hierarchy and the genocide of millions – was historical ignorance of the highest order. And, perhaps even more importantly, using it would only serve to alienate people, and curtail an important debate about whether we could afford to 'lend' more of our freedoms to the national effort to contain a deadly virus.

#ReclaimTheseStreets

Even with case rates and daily deaths rapidly falling, the police continued to treat outdoor protest as a criminal offence. On 7 March 2021, Karen Reissmann, a nurse and the organiser of a protest against a controversial 1 per cent rise in pay for NHS staff, was given a £10,000 Fixed Penalty Notice by the Greater Manchester Police. The outdoor rally had attracted around forty people.[8] I commented that the police had got it wrong and that reading the coronavirus regulations together with the Human Rights Act meant that socially distanced outdoor protest should be permitted.[9] Little did I realise that statement would be tested four days later with the entire country watching.

On Wednesday 3 March 2021, Sarah Everard, a 33-year-old marketing executive, disappeared while walking home from a friend's house near Clapham Common. Six days later, a serving Metropolitan Police officer, Wayne Couzens, was arrested on suspicion of kidnapping Sarah. He would later plead guilty to her kidnapping, rape and murder, and be sentenced with a whole life order, meaning he will almost certainly die in prison. During his sentencing, it was revealed that Couzens had cited COVID-19 laws to carry out a bogus 'arrest' of Sarah.

On 10 March, a newly formed women's safety collective, #ReclaimTheseStreets, announced on social media a vigil 'for all women threatened on our streets', to take place on Saturday 13 March on Clapham Common, close to where Sarah had gone missing. Immediately, Sarah's disappearance and the planned vigils attracted national attention – it was one of those moments which electrified everything; a horrific tragedy which ignited a movement. When it appeared that the women who were organising vigils were encountering resistance from the police, not just in London but from other forces across England, I offered on Twitter to give free advice to any organisers having difficulties. During the Thursday before the vigil, I spoke to a number of women who all told the same story. The police had initially been supportive of the vigils but at some point that day had changed their tune and were now saying the vigils would be illegal. Jessica Leigh, a local councillor and one of the organisers of the Clapham Common vigil, told me by telephone that she and her co-organisers had offered to use social distancing measures such as masks and QR codes, to no avail. By coincidence, that afternoon I was meeting a team of lawyers whom I had been working with on a different pandemic protest case.[10] This was fortuitous as the five of us understood the regulations and issues well already, and the team had a huge amount of protest and COVID-19 expertise. At the beginning of the meeting I suggested we take on Jessica and #ReclaimTheseStreets' case. Everyone was keen. We got to work on what would become one of the most important legal cases of the pandemic.

We decided that the first step would be to apply to the High Court for an urgent hearing the following day, Friday. We asked the court to rule that the Metropolitan Police's policy of treating all protest as illegal was itself a breach of the rights to freedom of speech and assembly protected by the Human Rights Act. But, at the hearing, the police told the court that was not, in fact, their policy.[11] The court decided not to make the ruling we had asked for – why would it, if the police had no such policy preventing all protest? Our clients met urgently with the police after the hearing, expecting that there would be a softening of their position. Surely, if a protest *could* be lawful, as the police told the court, then it was possible to find a version of the vigil which *would* be lawful? We assumed that the more measures in place to reduce the spread of COVID-19, the more likely the vigil would be lawful. But at the Friday night meeting, the police were unbending. They continued to threaten our clients with £10,000 FPNs and even prosecution under the Serious Crime Act for inciting others to commit offences under the coronavirus regulations.

After much agonising, the four organisers[12] made the decision to cancel. A vigil went ahead anyway, but not as they had planned – and without COVID-19 safety measures. The police intervened to break up the gathering, at times using physical force. The images of police violence were on the front page of every newspaper, with headlines such as 'SHAMING OF THE MET' accompanied by what became the iconic image of Patsy Stevenson, an attendee, forced onto the ground by police, hands held behind her back as she appeared to look up in terror.

The question was what to do next. The #ReclaimTheseStreets founders had pulled out, and exactly what they had predicted had happened – an unruly gathering which posed a serious COVID-19 risk, with everyone squeezed together to hear the speakers. The police response had appeared brutal, and it was lost on nobody that Sarah's (at the time, alleged) killer was a serving Metropolitan Police officer. How could women feel safe on the streets if their supposed protectors were themselves violent? Our clients decided to proceed with their legal case, to try to show that the police had acted unlawfully all along. It was not a straightforward decision – a case which had begun as being about women's rights to safety had also become about the right to free expression and protest during the pandemic. There were difficult moments in the coming months. We were struggling to finance the case through crowdfunding – although the organisation had received a huge amount of support, I imagine many wondered what the point was of the case continuing, given that the damage appeared to have been done after the brutal scenes at the vigil.

The full hearing in the case was held in January 2022. On 11 March 2022, two days before the anniversary of the vigil, the High Court ruled that the Metropolitan Police had acted unlawfully.[13] The key finding in the judgment was that the police could not do anything to enforce the coronavirus regulations without first carrying out a human rights proportionality assessment. And because the regulations were solely focused on protecting people from COVID-19, the police must make some assessment of the health risk, as weighed against the right to protest. If the gathering was for the purposes of protest on a political issue or some form of commemoration, the answer would not always be clearly against the holding of a gathering. The police, somewhat oddly, tried to argue that when they told the organisers that the vigil would be 'unlawful' or 'illegal', they did not actually mean it was a criminal offence – but the court rejected this. Ultimately, every time the police wrongly told the organisers that the vigil would necessarily be unlawful, it had a 'chilling effect on [the organisers'] exercise of their fundamental freedoms'.

The #ReclaimTheseStreets judgment came like a glass of cool water after almost two years of the courts rejecting cases on matters of COVID-19 policy. It may have helped that the threat of the virus seemed to have receded significantly by March 2022, therefore lowering the stakes if the court were to find against the Metropolitan Police. I do not know if such a judgment would have been possible during one of the surges in cases and deaths. But perhaps I am underestimating the principled objectivity of the judiciary even during the years of the Emergency State. On one view, the court had found that the police had been wrongly policing protest throughout the pandemic. This was an extraordinary outcome. It showed that what I and others suspected was true – the lockdown restrictions were being misinterpreted by the police, meaning people were prevented from lawfully exercising their right to protest freely. How could protest – the lifeblood of democracy – be banned for significant portions of a two-year period, without Parliament ever debating it or voting for it to happen, without any law explicitly decreeing it, merely through a 'misunderstanding' of the law by the police? This would have been unthinkable before the pandemic. The Emergency State had overwhelmed all the usual checks and balances – Parliament, the courts, public opinion – and this was one of the results.

To date, the government has not accepted that protests were wrongly policed, or that there was a breakdown in rights protection by every part of the state. There have been no reviews of Fixed Penalty Notices or prosecutions arising from protests. The #ReclaimTheseStreets judgment is of fundamental importance, but unless there is another lockdown its effect is retrospective only. Another important point is that the misunderstanding by the police resulted from the vague, ill-thought-through lockdown regulations. The vigil took place in March 2021, almost a year after the first lockdown law, so the novelty of the regulations was no excuse. I have no doubt that the breakneck pace of the changes to the legislation, and the failure to consult Parliament in any meaningful way, contributed to this disaster for rights. The police attempted twice to appeal the ruling but in May 2022 had their final appeal rejected.

Freedom day, or perhaps not

> [I]n my view the best response to [families'] grief and pain, and the sufferings that they have endured, is to get on . . . and roll out those vaccines and allow the people of this country to work forwards towards freedom day, which I devoutly hope will come on 19 July.
>
> Boris Johnson, 30 June 2021[14]

As spring turned to summer, the government's steps proceeded as planned, moving towards what the Prime Minister had with bombast and some hubris termed 'Freedom Day', 19 July, when the Steps regulations would be withdrawn and there would be, for the first time in the 480 days since 26 March 2020, no closed businesses, restrictions on gatherings, or stay-at-home orders.[15]

The Prime Minister had planned to summon 'the spirit of Churchill' with stirring rhetoric at an 'historic venue' associated with the Greatest Briton.[16] But it was always a mistake to frame the COVID-19 restrictions as an attack on freedom, as if *they* were the enemy. The enemy was COVID-19, even if *some* of the restrictions were unjustified. The Prime Minister may have seen freedom from the virus as a choice, a state of affairs which could be willed, a kind of test of national character – that he 'devoutly' hoped Freedom Day would come implied freedom could be the outcome of faith and prayer. And the invocation of Churchill was always problematic too. The Second World War involved a human enemy and a clear end point – celebrated as Victory in Europe Day – when it could conclusively be said the Nazis had been defeated. As we have seen, the Emergency State built during the Second World War had a long tail, and took many years after 1945 to dismantle. But it could confidently be said on VE Day that many of the most severe restrictions on freedom – curfews, requisition of property, the fear of invasion itself – ended. A pandemic has a different, more uncertain, lifespan, and it is unclear at best when we will no longer have to lend our freedoms to contain the spread of the virus by social distancing. The idea of a Freedom Day on 19 July was little more than wishful thinking, which also unhelpfully framed social distancing as a choice between freedom and unfreedom, as opposed to a choice between *different* freedoms – a choice to lend our social freedoms to protect public health and save lives. Agonisingly difficult choices are made harder by pretending there is a world where a deadly virus is uncontained yet life is lived normally and without risk.

And as if to prove that point, the virus took charge. Case rates were spiking and Sajid Javid, the new Health Secretary (Matt Hancock having resigned the previous month), tested positive for COVID-19, having come into recent close contact with the Prime Minister. I jokingly asked on Twitter whether ministers would suddenly be enrolled in a government experiment meaning they did not have to isolate. The following morning, Freedom Day Eve, it was reported that this would actually happen, as ministers would enrol in a 'trial testing scheme' and not self-isolate. As was common during the pandemic, fiction could barely keep up with fact. The decision was reversed within hours as a restive public, increasingly angry at the appearance that the government was not bothering to keep the rules they were setting for everyone else – whether Cummings' 'eye test', Hancock's affair or the Prime Minister reportedly not wanting to isolate – threatened to revolt. The Prime Minister would now spend Freedom Day in isolation at Chequers.[17]

The Omicron surge

It is hardly surprising that the public were confused if the government was framing the issue as one of freedom versus unfreedom, as opposed to a choice between freedoms while COVID-19 still posed a threat. Many would have expected Freedom Day to mean an end to all restrictions. That proved not to be even close to the case, as the legal requirement to self-isolate and international travel restrictions, including hotel quarantine, remained in place, and would do so until 18 March 2022, the second Freedom Day.

The prematurity of Freedom Day was highlighted in the winter of 2021, as the highly infectious Omicron variant arrived in the UK. Despite attempts to prevent the variant being imported, including an increase in countries on the travel red list, and therefore the numbers of people in hotel quarantine, it spread like wildfire.[18] Ministers reintroduced compulsory face coverings on public transport and in other settings,[19] COVID passes at larger gatherings and,[20] for a short period, compulsory isolation for people coming into contact with an Omicron case. There was to be no reintroduction of gathering restrictions or stay-at-home orders. But that did not mean 'freedom' had prevailed. From the beginning of December to early January 2022, positive test rates skyrocketed, well above anything seen before (although testing had not been as widely available in the earlier stages, meaning the comparisons with positive test results in 2020 are problematic). One of those positive tests was my own, as I had my first experience of the virus, along with the rest of my family in short succession. I had the strange experience of taking part in TV interviews about the new regulations from my home while unwell and feverish, trying to ensure that the words came out in the right order. There was a steep rise in infections throughout December, peaking on 4 January 2022 with over 275,000 cases identified on a single day. Over 15,000 people died in England after a positive COVID-19 test from mid-December 2021 to mid-March 2022, a three-month figure which at the beginning of the pandemic would have sounded unbelievable, a scare story. And yet by late 2021 this death rate was not deemed sufficient to impose harsher restrictions, even though such measures were being taken in other parts of the world facing Omicron, and indeed in other parts of the United Kingdom, such as Scotland, where large gatherings were limited, one-metre social distancing reimposed in indoor leisure settings and nightclubs closed.[21]

The huge rise in cases, exacerbated by the relatively modest restrictions, also led to what was described in the media as a 'pingdemic', a term first used in the summer of 2021 to describe the combination of high case rates with the legal requirement to self-isolate for ten days after testing positive.[22] In January 2022, there were potentially millions of people self-isolating, and therefore having to follow the strict self-isolation rules which did not even allow for exercise. Although, earlier in the pandemic, the High Court had found these rules not to meet the definition of 'imprisonment' or 'detention',[23] they were undoubtedly harsher than any of the various lockdown rules. A pingdemic which impacted millions of people and their families was in effect a lockdown by stealth – more targeted (and therefore more proportionate) but still a mass stay-at-home order enforced by the criminal law. In that sense, it is probably inaccurate to say that lockdowns ended with Freedom Day, 19 July – rather, they changed shape and were rebranded.

Partygate

> . . . better than them focusing on our drinks (which we seem to have got away with).
>
> Private message from Martin Reynolds, Principal Private Secretary to the Prime Minister[24]

The almost exponential rise in cases in December 2021 led, for a second year, to agonising over whether Christmas gatherings would be permitted. During that national conversation, a newspaper article appeared about parties that had occurred the year before, in November and December 2020. The *Daily Mirror* published a story by Pippa Crerar entitled 'Boris Johnson "broke Covid lockdown rules" with Downing Street parties at Xmas'.[25] The newspaper alleged that gatherings had taken place within the complex of buildings at No. 10 Downing Street, which also includes the Prime Minister's home, on 13 November (a leaving party, and a smaller gathering in the Prime Minister's flat), 27 November (another leaving party where the Prime Minister gave a speech) and 18 December (a full-blown Christmas party). A source told the newspaper that there were 'many social gatherings' in Downing Street while restrictions were in place and that there were 'always parties' in the Prime Minister's flat.

At a time when the risk of COVID-19 was again causing concern, the revelations were incendiary. A video was soon leaked of a mock press conference filmed on 22 December 2020 which showed the Prime Minister's then-spokesperson, Allegra

Stratton, responding to a question about 'a Downing Street Christmas party on Friday night'. 'I went home!' she said, before asking with seeming discomfort, 'What's the answer?'[26] One individual in the room suggested, 'It wasn't a party, it was cheese and wine.' Stratton responded, laughing, 'Is cheese and wine alright? It was a business meeting! This is recorded . . . this fictional party was a business meeting and it was not socially distanced.'

There were more reports of parties which had occurred from May 2020 to April 2021, many during lockdowns, including a large gathering in the Downing Street garden on 20 May 2020, during the first lockdown, where an email invitation from the Prime Minister's Principal Private Secretary suggested staff 'bring your own booze' for 'socially distanced drinks'. The Prime Minister himself had attended.

When Partygate happened, I realised that my coronavirus regulations spreadsheet, which I had hoped to mothball, was the only reliable way of finding out which laws applied to the ever-growing list of seemingly illegal Downing Street gatherings. It confirmed that the gatherings were potentially against the laws in place at the time. I was shocked that the gatherings had happened – they seemed such a brazen breach of both the regulations and guidance – but perhaps not as shocked as others were. The government had often acted in an opaque way during the pandemic, and there were indications it was abusing the enormous emergency powers granted to it, such as the grouse shooting story and the 'VIP lane'. There had already been multiple high-profile examples of rule-breaking behaviour by senior officials, such as by Dominic Cummings and Matt Hancock, accompanied by a willingness to cover up rule-breaking or bend the truth in relation to it. The Emergency State makes corruption more likely – it should not be a surprise when it is unearthed.

The revelations of what appeared to be straightforwardly

criminal behaviour kept coming, but the Metropolitan Police seemed curiously reluctant to investigate. On 8 December, the Met announced that, based on the 'absence of evidence' and 'in line with our policy not to investigate retrospective breaches' of coronavirus regulations, they would not commence an investigation. They appeared to be taking on trust the government's insistence that it had kept to the rules and guidance at all times, and were reassured that Simon Case, the country's most senior civil servant, had been appointed to investigate. But, on 17 December, Case had to recuse himself from the investigation because of allegations that a Christmas quiz had been held in his own office. He was replaced by Sue Gray, a senior civil servant who was well known in government circles as someone who could solve tough political problems.

But what was this supposed Met 'policy not to investigate retrospective breaches'? This had been mentioned in relation to Matt Hancock's indiscretions a few months earlier, but as far as I could tell the policy had never been published. It sounded a rather important document if it was determining whether the police investigated illegality at the heart of government. I was instructed by the Good Law Project to act in a judicial review of the Met's refusal to investigate,[27] and of its reliance on the secret 'no retrospective investigations policy'. The Met revealed its policy to us as part of the pre-action process. It turned out there *had* been a formal policy, and quite a sensible one. The problem was that it totally undermined the original decision not to investigate. It said that generally the Met would not investigate retrospective breaches of COVID-19 laws, but there was an exception for the most 'serious and flagrant' breaches where the suspect knew it was an offence or ought to have known, there was little ambiguity around any reasonable excuse, and not investigating would significantly undermine the legitimacy of the law. When it wrote the policy, the Met probably thought that there would be no cases which fell within this extremely narrow exception. And yet secret parties held at Downing Street, involving the *very people* who were drafting the coronavirus regulations, and even the Prime Minister himself, seemed to fit perfectly. The Good Law Project made these points in a judicial review issued on 17 January, and eight days later the Met reversed its decision, saying it would investigate the gatherings. Cressida Dick, the then-Commissioner of the Metropolitan Police, announced the U-turn at the London Assembly and read out the key parts of the retrospective investigations policy, explaining that the Met now considered there was enough evidence to investigate, having been handed evidence by Sue Gray. After the denials and evasions from the government and Prime Minister about whether any parties had taken place, the Met had decided that twelve separate gatherings appeared to be flagrant enough breaches that they would be investigated. The investigation would be named 'Op Hillman'.

Op Hillman concluded on 19 May 2022. One hundred and twenty-six Fixed Penalty Notices were issued relating to eight different gatherings – let's call them what they were: parties – which took place from May 2020 to April 2021, spanning each of the three national lockdowns. The fact that the police gave an FPN means that in each instance they believed a criminal offence had been committed. The Prime Minister received one FPN, for participating in a birthday party organised for him by his wife, Carrie Johnson, as did the Chancellor, Rishi Sunak.

Sue Gray reported on 25 May. She described boozy parties, subterfuge, leadership failings and a general culture of recklessness towards the rules that the people she was investigating had imposed on everyone else in the country. Although the details of the various parties had emerged via the press in the months prior to the report, there was still plenty of new information. In the lead-up to the notorious 20 May 2020 'bring your own booze' party, Lee Cain, the No. 10 Director of Communications, suggested to Boris Johnson's Principal Private Secretary, Martin Reynolds, that a '200 odd person invitation for drinks in the garden of no 10 is somewhat of a comms risk in the current environment'. After that party had taken place, Reynolds texted a special adviser about another story, of which he said 'better than them focusing on our drinks (which we seem to have got away with)'. At a party on 18 June 2020 involving pizza and prosecco, where the last person left after 3 a.m., Gray reported there was 'excessive alcohol consumption . . . One individual was sick. There was a minor altercation between two other individuals'. Helen MacNamara, Deputy Cabinet Secretary and previously Director-General for Propriety and Ethics, brought a karaoke machine. In the run-up to the party, staff messaged each other about 'drinks which aren't drinks' and tried to agree on an innocent-sounding name for the online diary invite. At a 15 December 2020 Christmas quiz, which the Prime Minister briefly attended, a No. 10 official sent a message on internal No. 10 systems referring to 'drunkenness' and advising staff to leave via the back exit to avoid being photographed by the press. A leaving party for Kate Josephs, a Director-General in the Covid Task Force (and therefore in charge of the COVID-19 regulations and guidance), involved more than twenty staff, food, alcohol and music, and ended after midnight. The 18 December 2020 Christmas party (the first to be reported by the *Daily Mirror*) had been organised weeks in advance, but the email invitation subject line had been changed from 'Wine & Cheese Evening' to 'End of Year Meeting with Wine & Cheese' – the exact ruse used by the No. 10 press officers when they giggled about the event in the leaked Allegra Stratton video.

Gray's report made No. 10 sound like an American college fraternity house rather than the nerve centre of the British government. There were multiple examples of 'a lack of respect and poor treatment of security and cleaning staff' – staff who, presumably, had to clean up the detritus and vomit after the late-night parties. There were 'failures of leadership and judgment'. Events should 'not have been allowed to happen' and some of the junior staff believed that their involvement in some of these events was permitted because 'their seniors were present, or indeed organised' the gatherings. Many members of the public, Gray suggested, would be 'dismayed that behaviour of this kind took place on this scale at the heart of Government'.

The BBC's *Panorama* programme interviewed three Downing Street staff involved in the parties. They described a toxic culture of rule-breaking, where raucous 'Wine-Time Friday' events happened every week from 4 p.m. and the Prime Minister watched on and sometimes participated because he 'wanted to be liked'.[28] When a member of the security staff tried to stop it all, 'people made fun of him because he was so worked up that this party was happening and it shouldn't be happening'. Everything just 'continued as normal', it wasn't 'like the outside world'. One former staffer said younger members of the team 'did not think they were breaking the rules at the time because the prime minister was at [the events], some of the most senior civil servants in the country were at them – and were indeed organising some of them'.

How did it happen that Downing Street, the heart of government, became one of the epicentres of criminal lockdown breaches during the pandemic? How was it *allowed* to happen? All three staffers paint a picture of Downing Street as a parallel universe. 'We saw it as our own bubble', said one, 'where the rules didn't really apply.' This gets to the heart of the matter. A key feature of the Emergency State is that power becomes overly concentrated among a small group of individuals. Who can withstand the pressure and the *temptations* of such power? The checks and balances, and transparency, which are features of democracies are intended to distribute power more widely and to withdraw temptations to corruption. We have learned these lessons through bitter experience, because every time power is given to too few people, the result is the same. From 2020 to 2021, No. 10 Downing Street became less like the office of the government in a democracy and more like the palace of a powerful monarch. Laws were passed by decree, without scrutiny; the ruler's hand was kissed as favours and patronage were handed out. And, in the meantime, the people who worked there quickly began to act like they were behind not the door of a democracy but the gate of a palace. They partied not because they were evil, or particularly decadent – I have no doubt they worked extremely hard – but because they thought they were *special*. They thought they lived in a parallel universe where the rules did not apply to them, just as behind every palace gate before them. And at the heart of it all was the ruler, who 'wanted to be liked', but who presided over – indeed, positively encouraged – a toxic culture where accountability was a word without meaning. A ruler who was ultimately brought down by a disregard for the rules that he spent two years encouraging – and forcing by law – the rest of the population to follow.

One staffer interviewed by the BBC was upset that people might look back at this period and think that the parties would define it, rather than the vaccine programme, or the food parcels for shielding people. But if we do not face the implications of the Emergency State, if we forget that there is a cost to power without scrutiny, what will *truly* define this era, along with 200,000 deaths and a dim memory of unbelievable events such as lockdowns, will be a failure to learn from our mistakes.

9. Freedom Regained?

When Parliament was faced, during the pandemic, with the excessive use of emergency powers under the Public Health Act, it made occasional noises but in the end might as well have prorogued itself for all the influence it had on the coronavirus regulations. The emergency procedure which avoided prior Parliamentary votes on legislation was used even when a policy had been trailed weeks earlier in the press, such as face coverings, COVID passes and hotel quarantine. Enormous, almost unimaginable, spending commitments were made which will take decades to pay back. And yet, out of over one hundred emergency regulations, many of them among the most controversial in history, Parliament could not point to a single one which was amended by a single word, let alone struck down. The voluminous laws which resulted were bloated and inconsistent, and often contradicted by official guidance and ministerial statements. This led directly to confusion and increasing desperation on the part of a public which was just trying to keep up, and to survive the crisis. In the courts, what few challenges were brought against the COVID-19 regulations failed, with judges making clear that the government has a wide discretion when making complex emergency decisions. The police floundered, given an impossible task, and failed to apply basic human rights standards which were required by law and could have made life under lockdown more humane. British society became as close to a police state as had occurred in living memory. Officials within the government, including the Prime Minister, behaved behind closed doors as if the rules which they were imposing by decree on the rest of the population did not apply to them, behaviour only exposed by diligent journalists and reluctant police, who only decided to investigate after being sued. These factors combined to produce the Emergency State – a bonfire of liberties stoked by an unaccountable executive.

The state of emergency formally ended with the repeal of the final travel regulations on 18 March 2022, over two years after it had been declared by Matt Hancock on Valentine's Day 2020.[1] I hesitate to write that these were the 'final' set of emergency regulations – there have been many false dawns already for the COVID-19 pandemic, and two editions of 'Freedom Day' so far. As it has become common to say: we may be done with Covid but Covid may not yet be done with us. If there is another variant of concern, or an unexpected surge in cases threatening to overwhelm health services, I am confident there will be further emergency regulations, and the cycle could begin again. It may be that there will be no more stay-at-home orders – but if there is one lesson of the last two years it is that there is a limit to what we as human societies can control. We may be at the beginning of the end of the COVID-19 pandemic or the end of the beginning. Either way, the end of the 763-day state of emergency, which became the Emergency State, offers an important opportunity to reflect. It should also be a wake-up call, because some of the corrosive effects on our democracy have been gestating for years – they are not unique to the pandemic.

Nobody planned the COVID-19 Emergency State – we were thrown into it. When Parliament amended the Public Health Act in 2008, MPs and members of the Lords did not anticipate that regulations made under it would be used to lock down the entire country for months, even less that there would be stay-at-home or gathering restrictions for 480 days, and that the emergency procedure would be used for 763 days to prevent Parliament from having a prior vote or debating on nearly all of the over one hundred changes to the regulations from 2020 to

2022. This is not a criticism of Parliament for being unprepared or failing to see the writing on the wall. In March 2020, national lockdowns were essentially new – I have only been able to find previous examples for five days in Mexico in 2009 and three days in Sierra Leone in 2014. So when China imposed a lockdown in Wuhan in January 2020, and within weeks most of the world followed, the aggressiveness of the measures was unprecedented and largely untested. It is therefore difficult to criticise the UK's government, or its Parliament, for not anticipating, preparing for or properly understanding the implications of national lockdowns. The UK was swept up by the centrifugal force of the worldwide movement towards lockdowns, which we must also remember was supported and encouraged by the World Health Organization, the United Nations and even the Pope.

It is fascinating to wonder what would have happened if the pandemic had started in liberal, democratic Western Europe rather than authoritarian China. Would national lockdowns, backed up by the full force of state security, have spread as they did in March 2020? We will never know, but we must at least recognise that while social distancing measures, curfews and travel bans are likely to have been imposed, as they had been during plague outbreaks for centuries, indiscriminate stay-at-home orders were not inevitable. It is also important to recognise that although most states implemented what they termed 'lockdowns', the strictness of these varied widely. At least compared to other large Western European states, the UK lockdown seems to have been enforced with a lighter touch. And China used – and still uses – measures such as quarantine centres (known as *fangcang* facilities) for all those infected with or known to have had contact with a case of COVID-19, essentially detention centres, which have not been implemented in other states.[2] Not all lockdowns were equal – there were and remain wide variations in policies, which make direct comparison a risky business.

It is the case that once stay-at-home orders became the internationally accepted model for tackling the COVID-19 outbreak, states would have to implement them with whatever emergency response mechanisms they happened to have in place in March 2020, and whichever leader was unlucky enough to be in office would have to manage the fallout. Aristotle described a tragic hero as a man who is otherwise favoured, but suffers from an inherent character flaw. This flaw, when combined with extraordinary events, leads to disaster and ultimately his downfall.[3] States of emergency are extreme circumstances that are bound to expose any inherent flaw in the state or those who happen to be in charge of it at the time. 'Like many large organisations,' said Iain Martin in *The Times* in the wake of the Sue Gray report, 'governments tend to reflect the personality of the individual running them', and this 'tends to apply even more in our relatively uncodified system'. The British style of government 'works only when the person at the top knows what they are doing'.[4]

When the COVID-19 pandemic reached our shores, Boris Johnson's government had only been in power for a few months but had already attempted, and failed, to shut down Parliament for weeks so it could ram through a Brexit deal. The tragic flaw in Johnson's government, and arguably in him, was that it saw Parliamentary democracy as an inconvenience, a gadfly to be swatted away. When faced with the magnitude of the COVID-19 crisis, no doubt many leaders worldwide felt the temptation to do the same. But a combination of factors in the UK – too-permissive public health legislation, which was never designed to implement lockdowns and which was essentially overwhelmed by them; a submissive Parliament; weak legal protections; and politicians who saw the democratic process not as an opportunity but a hindrance, and who were so lacking in integrity that they held multiple illegal parties within Downing

Street during the lockdowns – enabled the Johnson government to take the reins from Parliament and not give them back for over two years.

The Public Health Act is a flawed piece of legislation which made it too easy for a government to legislate without accountability. The Civil Contingencies Act, which according to Dominic Cummings was bypassed to avoid the risk of litigation, also gives the government immense power but has stronger safeguards. It would have required the government to bring regulations to Parliament within seven days, instead of twenty-eight, or they would automatically lapse, and even then they would only last for thirty days. It also includes strong provision in case Parliament is prorogued when the regulations are brought before it. It allows for more robust scrutiny. Crucially, it permits Parliament to amend regulations, which should be a right not a privilege when it comes to laws which remove important rights.

I am not suggesting that emergency law-making would ever be straightforward and neat, following all the processes of ordinary legislation. Public emergencies are times of challenge for the state. Events move swiftly and mercilessly. But it did not have to be like *this*. The approach of the devolved legislature in Scotland, which made its own, separate, COVID-19 policy, has been described by legal academics as 'impressive (though imperfect) political accountability characterised by openness and transparency by the government, cross-party collaboration, and energetic Parliamentary committees performing high quality scrutiny'.[5] In Finland, there was 'real-time' Parliamentary scrutiny of the constitutionality and human rights compliance of COVID-19 regulations. In Sweden, a cross-party Parliamentary commission was set up to review the actions of government during the pandemic. In Singapore, the extension of any emergency powers had to be made by Parliament as opposed to the Minister of Health. The approach of New Zealand, which like

Sweden had a formal 'Continuous Improvement' process of external oversight of COVID-19 policy, may, according to academics Joelle Grogan and Julinda Beqiraj, 'prove exemplary' in ensuring democratic and constitutional accountability as well as learning from experience.[6]

By contrast, the UK Parliament had a number of Parliamentary committees, such as the Joint Committee on Human Rights which I worked on, yet the government could (and often did) ignore their findings. There was also no organised scrutiny or independent reviewer of policing in England. This was a huge mistake which I have no doubt allowed clanging errors to occur, such as that which the High Court identified in the #Reclaim TheseStreets case. In Scotland and Northern Ireland, however, independent reviewers[7] were appointed and reported regularly.[8]

Another enabling factor was the constant refrain that the government was 'following the science', by which it meant its scientific advisory group, SAGE, which *itself* was admirably transparent through its publication of minutes and papers. But the reality was that SAGE made recommendations and the government then decided on detailed policy, sometimes following recommendations and sometimes not. Those decisions were taken in the extremely powerful but entirely opaque COVID-19 cabinet committees, presided over by four ministers. No minutes were released and no explanation offered of how decisions were taken, except for occasional leaks when there was a disagreement. This Covid Politburo was the most powerful government committee since the Second World War, but received no scrutiny at all. The 'following the science' mantra was comforting, as it made it seem as if decisions were being made on an objective basis, and probably reassured people that even if Parliament was more involved, it would be redundant as it would follow the science too. But this was false reassurance. The courts had it right by categorising policy decisions as ultimately political, although taken on the basis of scientific advice. Important political decisions need to be understood, scrutinised and tested. The COVID-19 cabinet committees were the nerve centre of the Emergency State but they became a democratic black box – inaccessible and secretive.

We cannot go back in time to see our relatives as they were dying in hospital, or to worship together during the darkest days, or to exercise our right to protest. And as I have explored, some of those freedoms were lent for good reason, to save the lives of those who were vulnerable to COVID-19. The extent to which particular freedoms should never have been restricted, or been given back sooner, are questions with no easy answer. As tempting as it is to take a simplified position – to say, as Lord Sumption did, that restrictions should only have been voluntary – I believe that it was necessary for states to put in place some temporary measures to protect citizens from an unknown disease which was threatening to overwhelm health services and hundreds of thousands of people.

But it would be a mistake to think that when the state of emergency ended on 18 March 2022, everything returned to normal. We still live in the state which permitted ministers to rule by decree for over two years. Unless we use this hiatus to claw back some of our democratic rights, another Emergency State will emerge, perhaps a worse one. It is only a matter of time before a new crisis will arise – either connected to COVID-19 (which is stubbornly resisting the government's hopeful diagnosis that it has disappeared as a threat),[9] to another virus or to another kind of emergency altogether. Perhaps some form of Emergency State is inevitable during a true national emergency, an existential threat. But we must do everything we can to mitigate the costs which I identified in Chapter 1 – over-concentration of power, ignorant decision-making caused by the weakening of the usual democratic institutions, corruption and the tendency to self-reinforce, with the effects persisting well beyond the emergency itself.

There was no magic policy whereby the spread of COVID-19 could have been limited without any trade-offs of our freedoms. As was the refrain during the Second World War, states of emergency require that liberties are *lent* for the greater good. And over thousands of years we have unfortunately found no better way to prevent the spread of a highly contagious disease, for which there is no cure, than enforced social distancing through curfews, closing pubs and schools, banning gatherings, quarantining the potentially infectious and isolating the known infectious. Modern science has resulted in better treatment and prevention of plagues through vaccinations. But in the early stages of a pandemic, when science has not yet come to the rescue, we are forced to resort to the centuries-old methods. It is beyond the scope of this book to reach a scientific conclusion as to which methods should have been used and which not. But it is clear enough to me, even without scientific expertise, that some kind of enforced social distancing was unavoidable. A crucial question for the future is whether national stay-at-home orders – which, as I have shown, are a *new* innovation probably made feasible only because of the rise of the internet, which allowed many to work, communicate and learn at home – justified the enormous collateral damage which they caused. It is possible, however, to insulate ourselves better from the Emergency State rearing its head again, either in the next stage of the COVID-19 pandemic or during the next pandemic. In that respect, I have four suggestions.

First, the powers under the Public Health Act must be given equivalent safeguards to those under the Civil Contingencies Act. Regulations should lapse if they are not voted in by Parliament within seven days, and should last only thirty days unless reinstated by a further set of regulations, which likewise would need to be approved within seven days. It makes no sense for some vast emergency powers to require more scrutiny and caution than others. Crucially, Parliament needs to be allowed to amend emergency regulations. Without that power, Parliamentarians are left with the choice of either passing or rejecting regulations, which during an emergency is often no choice at all. Drafts of regulations should also be published in advance so that Parliament can properly consider them. Parliament could have been involved more, even given the urgency of policy-making during the COVID-19 pandemic: the government could have published drafts of legislation in advance, or set up a special committee to scrutinise laws and the policies behind them; it could have published minutes of its Covid Strategy Committee meetings; it could have invited leaders of opposition parties to those meetings. No aspect of the Public Health Act *prevented* transparency and accountability. But it was a law which was open to abuse by a government with little regard for democratic process.

Second, all prosecutions under the coronavirus regulations and all Fixed Penalty Notices should be reviewed. The #ReclaimTheseStreets case, as well as the many incidents reported in this book, clearly demonstrate that the police did not fully understand the laws they were enforcing. Whatever the reason, many sanctions were wrongly handed out. Some people will have unnecessarily paid thousands of pounds in fines, others will have a criminal record. The hidden injustices of the pandemic must be brought into the light.

Third – and this is the big one – we should start working towards a codified constitution, or at the least a genuine bill of rights with real teeth. One of the terrifying aspects of the COVID-19 pandemic was the way in which freedoms were taken away without due process. The famous 'checks and balances' of Parliament and the courts were largely absent, despite ancient freedoms such as the right to worship in public and the right to protest being removed for months at a time. The courts did intervene, in Scotland over worship and in England over protest – but only after the event.[10] This should be a stark warning. The courts were generally keen to stay out of what they saw as complex policy decisions. But these were not just government policy decisions, they also profoundly curtailed our rights. One of the fundamental weaknesses of our unwritten or uncodified constitution is that states of emergency do not have clear rules or time limits, as they generally do under codified constitutional systems, where if there are going to be emergency limits on certain rights those limits should be clearly set out and themselves *limited*. Then it is up to the courts to ensure that the government adheres to those limits and, and if it doesn't adhere, the courts have the power to strike down laws. Having said that, the courts could already have struck down any aspect of the coronavirus regulations if they had breached the Human Rights Act. But they simply did not see it as their role to do so because of what they understood to be the UK's delicate constitutional balance, where Parliament tends to call the shots over sensitive public policy choices.

It has become fashionable in recent years to claim that judges have too much power in our political system and that the Human Rights Act and judicial review have encouraged the courts to become too involved in politics. This was exemplified by the *Daily Mail*'s 2016 'ENEMIES OF THE PEOPLE' headline, accompanied by the mugshots of three judges who had decided that the consent of Parliament was needed before the government triggered the UK leaving the European Union. More recently, the UK government, resentful of the Supreme Court's ruling in 2019 that the government's attempt to temporarily shut down Parliament was unlawful, has launched a multi-pronged attack on the ability of citizens to challenge unlawful government decisions. After weakening judicial review through new legislation, it has turned its aim on the Human Rights Act, which the government proposes to replace with a new 'Bill of Rights', though in truth the proposed bill of rights would be the first in the history of democracy to weaken rather than strengthen protections. This is a government which has shown time and again that it is contemptuous of courts – and 'left-wing' lawyers for that matter, whom ministers regularly blame for policies going wrong. But they have it the wrong way round. Courts, and citizens' ability to challenge unlawful government actions, should be *strengthened*. In a liberal state, courts should be seen as a partner in the democratic process, not a hindrance or even an enemy. A codified constitution would not solve every problem (and would create a few of its own, such as judges becoming more politicised), but it would at least make the division of power between the institutions of the state clearer and ensure that courts can act as a genuine check on the actions of the executive, a role which becomes even more essential during a state of emergency.

Fourth, human rights need to be placed at the heart of government decision-making during a state of emergency. As we saw, the European Convention on Human Rights was forged from the fires of the Second World War and the Holocaust, to act as an early warning system for tyranny in Europe. Not all tyranny looks the same. It may arrive with the sound of fascist jackboots, but it can also appear in the guise of emergency laws, the over-concentration of power and, as Orwell put it, the 'general temper in the country', where dissent is squashed and groupthink becomes common – *we want it to happen*. In other words, the Emergency State. This is what human rights are *for*. They exist to protect against the overbearing state. Recall the words of Pierre-Henri Teitgen: 'evil progresses cunningly . . . one by one freedoms are suppressed' while 'public opinion and the entire national conscience are asphyxiated'.

The essential truth is that if we look out only for fascism or totalitarianism in its final form, it may be too late to stop it. Many rights in the European Convention on Human Rights, such as the right to freedom of expression, the right to private and family life and the right to practise a religion, are designed so that they can be interfered with if that interference is proportionate. No individual is an island and liberal societies must often negotiate between different groups' entitlement to rights, as well as imposing responsibilities. It is therefore wrong to see freedom as something which is switched on or off – freedom exists on a continuum and what it looks like for any individual will depend in part on the circumstances of the time. Human rights laws are carefully designed to act as a warning system to ensure that rights are not unnecessarily removed during the inevitable chaos caused by a national emergency. They should be more explicitly built into all emergency legislation.

Diagnosing the disease

The COVID-19 pandemic and the rise of the Emergency State have been national traumas from which we are only beginning to recover, if indeed they are over at all. We have over 200,000 dead and many others suffering from the long-lasting effects of COVID-19. The UK's death rate as a percentage of the population is the seventh highest in the world and the third highest in Western Europe, suggesting that something in the way the government handled the pandemic may have gone badly wrong.[11] We are a country – and a world – traumatised by the most consequential pandemic in a hundred years. Attention will rightly be focused on the public health interventions we and many other countries used: did they work, what was the collateral damage, were they made too late or too soon, too hard or not hard enough? There are few if any straightforward answers to those questions. But we must also focus on questions which go the heart of the way our country is run. The executive is increasingly powerful in normal times.[12] In times of emergency, however, our current laws, combined with deference in the courts and an uncodified, disorganised and dishevelled constitution, allow ministers to act like dictators. This is bad for the quality of policies, as the healthy challenge of a functioning democracy disappears; and it is terrible for rights, because authoritarianism inevitably leads to discrimination and corruption.

It's not all bad. We did not slide into a dictatorship during the COVID-19 years, and much can be repaired. It feels meaningful that at the same moment I finished the draft of this book I watched Boris Johnson announce his resignation as Prime Minister, brought down in large part due to the exposure of illegal behaviour behind the palace gates, as Matt Hancock and Dominic Cummings, two other key architects of the Emergency State, had been before him. Just because a government tries to behave like authoritarians doesn't mean we will let them. Or perhaps, more accurately, it doesn't mean there will be no consequences once the emergency has passed and ordinary democratic business resumes.

C. K. Allen, scholar of emergency powers under the Second World War, reminds us that freedom 'is not easily gained, and, once surrendered – however necessary the surrender may be – is even less easily regained'. A state of emergency does not necessarily lead to the Emergency State. For 763 days, between 2020 and 2022, it did. But its worst excesses can still be curbed and the most important benefits of democracy preserved. If we can accurately diagnose the disease, it is possible, in time, to find the treatment – and maybe even a cure.

Acknowledgements

I would not have been able to write this book without the support of my wonderful family, and particularly my wife, Julia, who is the wisest and best person I know. And of my parents, who have been there for me at every step of the way. I have been greatly assisted in researching the book by Claudia Hyde. Thank you to my agent, Antony Topping, who has patiently encouraged me, over years now, to write a book, and then to write this book. To Stuart Williams and the staff at The Bodley Head, who made helpful suggestions and ably shepherded me through the writing process. To my colleagues and the staff at Doughty Street Chambers, who have been greatly supportive and inspiring throughout the pandemic. To Yoav Segal, who gave sage advice, as always, on design. Finally, to the lawyers and academics on Twitter, who have hugely assisted me in understanding and disseminating the COVID-19 laws, always ready to dive into an obscure bit of legal drafting, sometimes late at night. You have all made me a better lawyer, even (perhaps especially) the ones who argue with me, and perform a major public service by helping people to understand the law.

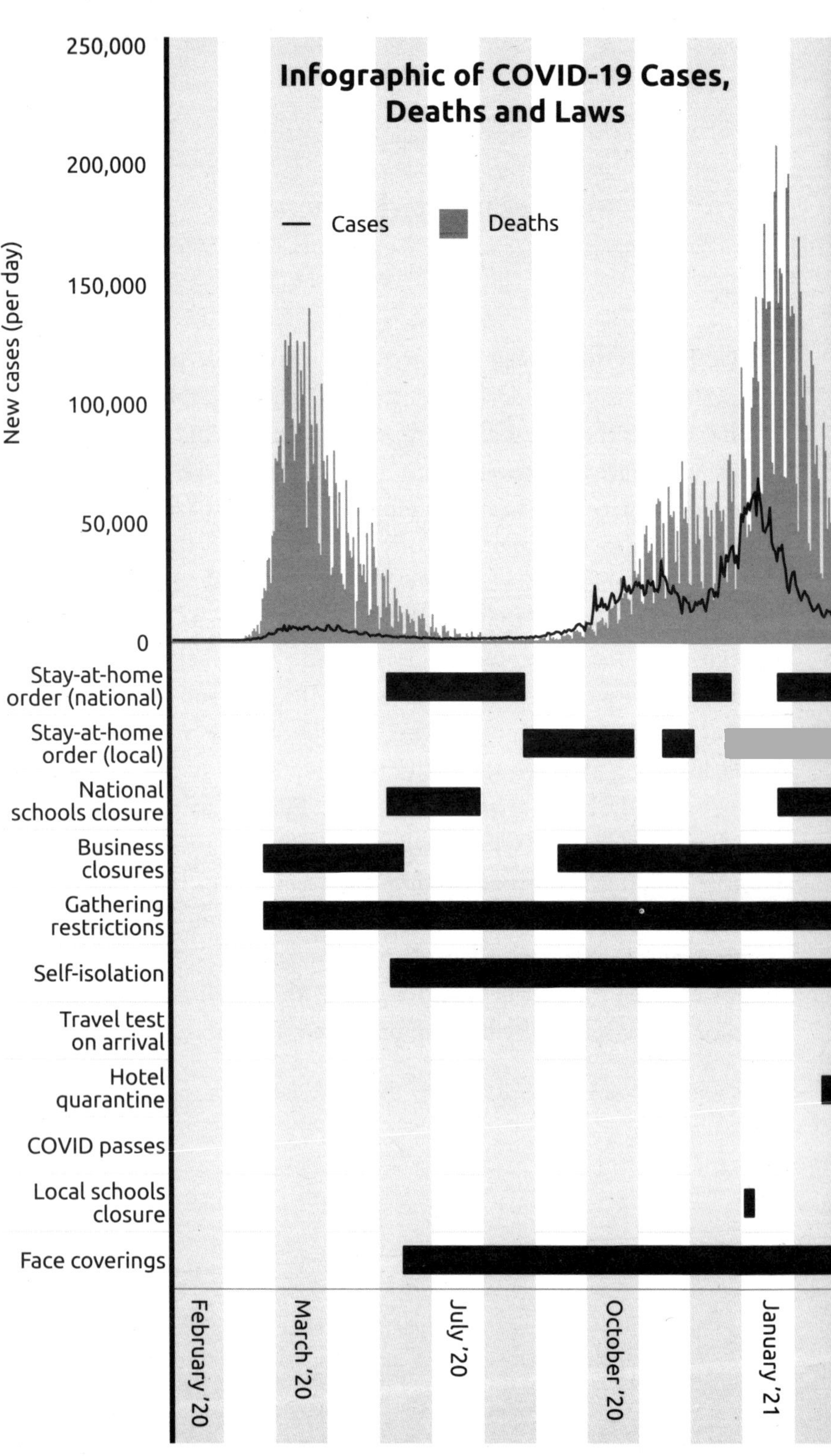
Infographic of COVID-19 Cases, Deaths and Laws
Cases
Deaths
New cases (per day)
250,000
200,000
150,000
100,000
50,000
0
Stay-at-home order (national)
Stay-at-home order (local)
National schools closure
Business closures
Gathering restrictions
Self-isolation
Travel test on arrival
Hotel quarantine
COVID passes
Local schools closure
Face coverings
February '20
March '20
July '20
October '20
January '21

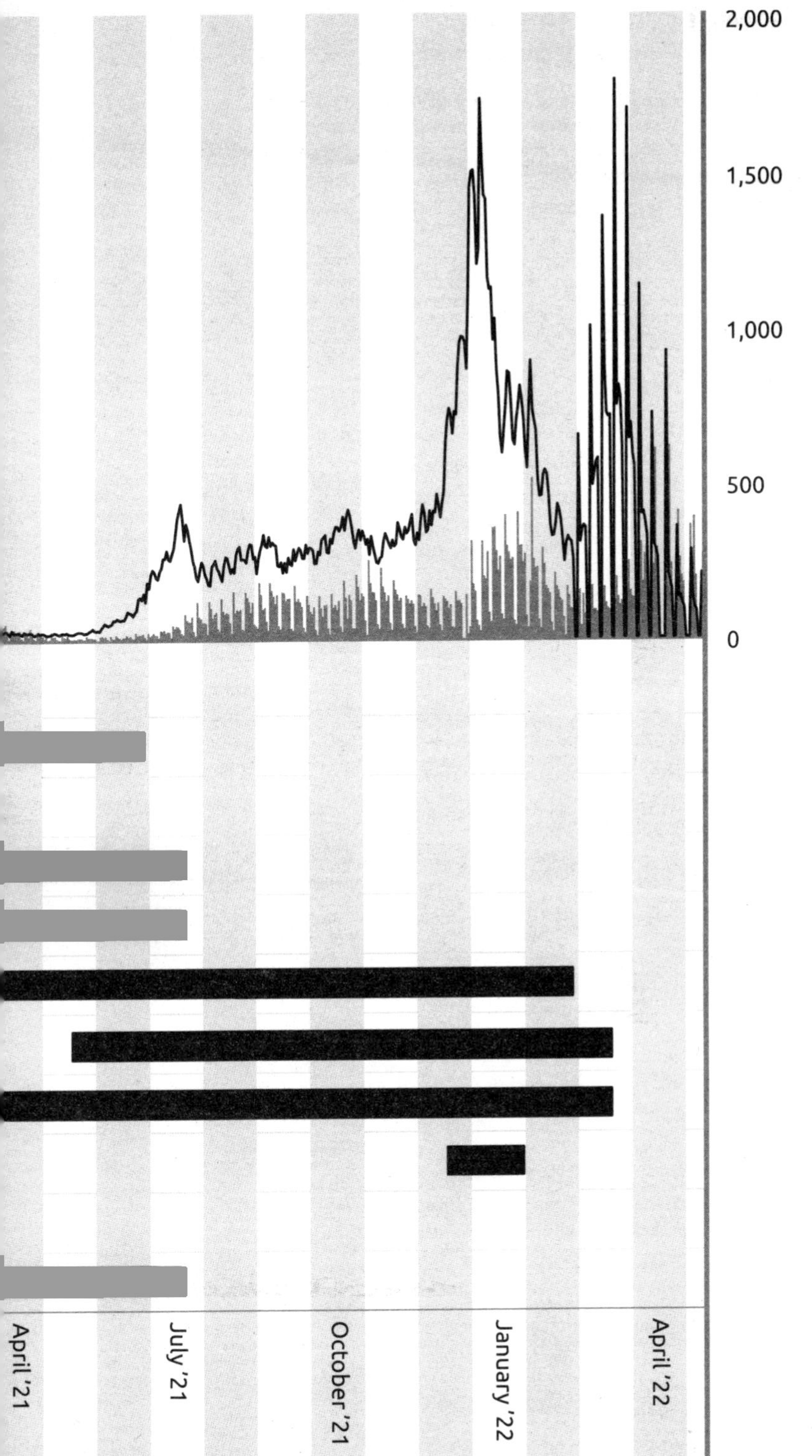
2,000
1,500
1,000
500
0
New deaths (per day)
April '21
July '21
October '21
January '22
April '22

Timeline of COVID-19 Laws

2020

14 February

'Serious and imminent threat' declaration made and first set of travel regulations triggered

26 March

First national lockdown law comes into force

Schools shut for most children

1 June

Leaving home restrictions removed

Rule of six outdoors

Gatherings of more than one person indoors banned

15 June

Face coverings mandated on public transport

Linked households (support bubbles) introduced

4 July

First local lockdown imposed in Leicester, further local lockdowns to follow in other areas

4 July

National lockdown relaxed, pubs opened, larger gatherings to follow guidance

12 April

Step 2

Restaurants and other hospitality allowed to open for outdoor seating, gyms re-opened

17 May

Step 3

Groups of thirty allowed outdoors, mixing indoors with up to six or two households, international travel permitted in law without 'reasonable excuse'

18 June

Steps regulations revoked ending legal limits on gatherings

16 August

Double-vaccinated adults and all children no longer need to self-isolate when in contact with positive case

1 October

Green and amber lists no longer part of travel regulations

30 November

Close contacts of people with Omicron variant have to isolate whether or not vaccinated

'Plan B' begins with face covering regulations reintroduced

15 December

COVID passes introduced

18 July

Local authorities given powers to close businesses and impose restrictions

28 August

£10,000 Fixed Penalty Notice introduced for raves and gatherings over thirty

14 September

Rule of six introduced nationally, no mingling, support groups permitted, significant event gatherings, grouse shooting

28 September

Legal duty to self-isolate imposed

14 October

'Three tiers' regulations introduced

5 November

Second national lockdown imposed

Schools remain open

2 December

New three tiers

'Linked Christmas Households' introduced

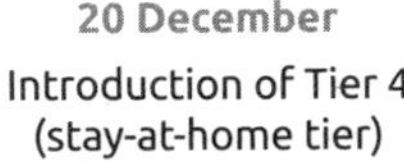

20 December

Introduction of Tier 4 (stay-at-home tier)

6 January

Third national lockdown

Schools closed

15 February

Hotel quarantine introduced

29 March

Step 1

Rule of six outdoors, no international travel without reasonable excuse

2022

26 January

Plan B (COVID passes and face coverings) ends

18 March

Last remaining coronavirus regulations (travel) revoked, ending 763-day state of emergency and rule by ministerial decree

Notes

Preface

1 'Prime Minister's statement on coronavirus (COVID-19): 23 March 2020', www.gov.uk/government/speeches/pm-address-to-the-nation-on-coronavirus-23-march-2020.

2 Civil Contingencies Act 2004, section 1.

3 The Public Health (Control of Disease) Act 1984, which was the legal basis of The Health Protection (Coronavirus, Business Closure) (England) Regulations 2020, brought into force on 21 March 2020.

4 The Health Protection (Coronavirus, Restrictions) (England) Regulations 2020, UKSI 2020/350.

5 'Fixed Penalty Notices (FPNs) issued under COVID-19 emergency health regulations by police forces in England and Wales', NPCC, 16 March 2022, cdn.prgloo.com/media/d0f7e8f380ad402ea48e70a85bc389eb.pdf.

6 'CPS review findings for first year of coronavirus prosecutions', Crown Prosecution Service, 13 May 2021, www.cps.gov.uk/cps/news/cps-review-findings-first-year-coronavirus-prosecutions.

7 '14.9 million excess deaths associated with the COVID-19 pandemic in 2020 and 2021', World Health Organization, 5 May 2022, www.who.int/news/item/05-05-2022-14.9-million-excess-deaths-were-associated-with-the-covid-19-pandemic-in-2020-and-2021.

8 Deaths with COVID-19 on the death certificate, coronavirus.data.gov.uk/details/deaths.

9 docs.google.com/document/d/1ne4zhPYAZK8G867D1Iz0Gg2ZJFLGmF2K/edit.

1. States of Emergency

1 Adam Gopnik, *A Thousand Small Sanities: The Moral Adventure of Liberalism* (London, 2020), p. 80.

2 Carleton Kemp Allen, *Law and Orders: An Inquiry into the Nature and Scope of Delegated Legislation and Executive Powers in England* (London, 1965), p. 64.

3 John Henley, 'Democratic leaders win surge of approval during Covid-19 crisis', *Guardian*, 2 April 2020, www.theguardian.com/world/2020/apr/02/democratic-leaders-win-surge-of-approval-during-covid-19-crisis.

4 Jonathan Haidt, *The Righteous Mind: Why Good People are Divided by Politics and Religion* (London, 2013), p. 276.

5 Alaa Elassar, ' "Those people are not me": US Muslims reflect on how 9/11 changed their lives and what the future holds for them', CNN, 10 September 2021, edition.cnn.com/2021/09/07/us/muslims-relationship-with-america-september-11/index.html.

6 See, for example, the JUSTICE summary: 'Counter-terrorism and human rights', justice.org.uk/counter-terrorism-human-rights.

7 Orwell was responding to the arrest for 'obstruction' of five people for selling anarchist newspapers outside Hyde Park. George Orwell, 'Freedom of the Park', *Tribune*, 7 December 1945, www.orwellfoundation.com/the-orwell-foundation/orwell/essays-and-other-works/freedom-of-the-park.

2. Very Strong Measures

1 The case and deaths data at the beginnings of chapters are for the United Kingdom and are taken from https://coronavirus.data.gov.uk/details/deaths.

2 WHO, 'Novel Coronavirus (2019-nCoV) Situation Report – 1', 21 January 2020, www.who.int/docs/default-source/coronaviruse/situation-reports/20200121-sitrep-1-2019-ncov.pdf.

3 As reported by Geoff Manaugh and Nicola Twilley in their *Until Proven Safe: The History and Future of Quarantine* (London, 2021), p. 8.

4 James Griffiths and Amy Woodyatt, 'China goes into emergency mode as number of confirmed Wuhan coronavirus cases reaches 2,700', CNN, 27 January 2020, edition.cnn.com/2020/01/26/asia/wuhan-coronavirus-update-intl-hnk/index.html.

5 The International Health Regulations are an international legal agreement that all 196 parties to the WHO have signed up to; see www.who.int/publications/i/item/9789241580496.

6 IHR 2005, Annex 2.

7 'Statement on the second meeting of the International Health Regulations (2005) Emergency Committee regarding the outbreak of novel coronavirus (2019-nCoV)', 30 January 2020, www.who.int/news/item/30-01-2020-statement-on-the-second-meeting-of-the-international-health-regulations-(2005)-emergency-committee-regarding-the-outbreak-of-novel-coronavirus-(2019-ncov).

8 'Pope Francis praises China's efforts to contain coronavirus', Reuters, 26 January 2020, www.reuters.com/article/us-china-health-pope/pope-francis-praises-chinas-efforts-to-contain-coronavirus-idUSKBN1ZP0EP.

9 'Statement from the 4 UK Chief Medical Officers on novel coronavirus', 30 January 2020, www.gov.uk/government/news/statement-from-the-four-uk-chief-medical-officers-on-novel-coronavirus.

10 'Coronavirus: two cases confirmed in UK', BBC News, 31 January 2020, www.bbc.co.uk/news/health-51325192.

11 'SPI-M-O: Consensus Statement on 2019 Novel Coronavirus (2019-nCoV)', UK Scientific Pandemic Influenza Modelling Committee, 10 February 2020, assets.publishing.service.gov.uk/government/uploads/system/uploads/attachment_data/file/882713/17-spi-m-o-consensus-statement-10022020.pdf.

12 The Health Protection (Coronavirus) Regulations 2020, UKSI 2020/129.

13 'What is Secondary Legislation?', UK Parliament website, www.parliament.uk/about/how/laws/secondary-legislation.

14 Parliament's website reports that around 3,500 are made each year but only around 1,000 need to be considered by Parliament, https://www.parliament.uk/about/how/laws/secondary-legislation/.

15 UK Parliament website, www.parliament.uk/about/how/laws/secondary-legislation.

16 www.legislation.gov.uk/ukpga/1984/22/contents.

17 Luke Kemp, 'The "Stomp Reflex": when governments abuse emergency powers', BBC, 28 April 2021, www.bbc.com/future/article/20210427-the-stomp-reflex-when-governments-abuse-emergency-powers.

18 W. Smith, W. Wayte and G. E. Marindin, *A Dictionary of Greek and Roman Antiquities* (London, 1890), p. 1052.

19 D. B. Nagle, 'The failure of the roman political process in 133 B.C.', *Athenaeum*, 49, 1971, pp. 111–28.

20 Wilfried Nippel, 'Emergency Powers in the Roman Republic', in P. Pasquino and B. Manin (eds.), *La théorie politico-constitutionnelle du gouvernement d'exception* (Palaiseau, 2000).

21 Those states were Romania, Armenia, Moldova, Estonia, Georgia, Albania, North Macedonia, Serbia, San Marino and Latvia, all of which derogated in March and April 2020; see 'Derogations by States Parties from Article 21 ICCPR, Article 11 ECHR, and Article 15 ACHR on the Basis of the COVID-19 Pandemic', 3 March 2021, www.rightofassembly.info/assets/downloads/Derogations_by_States_Parties_from_the_right_to_assembly_on_the_Basis_of_the_COVID_19_Pandemic_(as_of_3_March_2021).pdf.

22 Allen, p. 63.

23 Hansard, HC Debate, 18 December 1945. The example case is taken from the debate.

24 Incidentally, he was the British prosecutor at the Nuremberg trials for the prosecution of Nazi leaders in 1945–6, along with David Maxwell Fyfe, who will be mentioned later in relation to the European Convention on Human Rights.

25 *Liversidge v Anderson* [1941], www.bailii.org/uk/cases/UKHL/1941/1.html.

26 Hansard, HC Debate, 24 November 1953.

27 In the decision granting permission to appeal to the Court of Appeal in *Dolan & Ors, R (On the Application Of) v The Secretary of State for Health and Social Care & Anor* [2020] EWCA Civ 1605, static.crowdjustice.com/crowdjustice_document/Court_of_Appeals_Order_-_4_August_2020.pdf.

28 As Lord Morpeth said when introducing the bill for the government: HC Debate, 10 February 1848, vol. 96, cols 386–7.

29 See sections 19 and 21.

30 Russell T Davies, 'I looked away for years. Finally, I have put Aids at the centre of a drama', *Guardian*, 3 January 2021, www.theguardian.com/tv-and-radio/2021/jan/03/russell-t-davies-i-looked-away-for-years-finally-i-have-put-aids-at-the-centre-of-a-drama.

31 The Public Health (Infectious Diseases) Regulations 1985, UKSI 1985/434.

32 'AIDS victim ordered confined under new law', United Press International, 15 September 1985, www.upi.com/Archives/1985/09/15/AIDS-victim-ordered-confined-under-new-law/4382495604800.

33 'Superbia Spotlights: It's A Sin . . . Manchester's unique HIV & AIDS legacy', 9 February 2021, www.manchestersfinest.com/articles/superbia-spotlights-its-a-sin-manchesters-unique-hiv-aids-legacy.

34 United Nations, 'Constitution of the World Health Organization: New York, 22 July 1946'. Available at treaties.un.org/Pages/ShowMTDSGDetails.aspx?src=UNTSONLINE&tabid=2&mtdsg_no=IX-1&chapter=9&lang=en.

35 'China's latest SARS outbreak has been contained, but biosafety concerns remain – update 7', World Health Organization, 18 May 2004, www.who.int/emergencies/disease-outbreak-news/item/2004_05_18a-en.

36 James Pasley, 'How SARS terrified the world in 2003, infecting more than 8,000 people and killing 774', Markets Insider, 20 February 2020, markets.businessinsider.com/news/stocks/deadly-sars-virus-history-2003-in-photos-2020-2.

37 Yanzhong Huang, 'The SARS epidemic and its aftermath in China: a political perspective', in S. Knobler et al. (eds.), *Learning from SARS: Preparing for the Next Disease Outbreak: Workshop Summary*, Institute of Medicine (US) Forum on Microbial Threats (Washington, DC, 2004). Available online at www.ncbi.nlm.nih.gov/books/NBK92479.

38 International Health Regulations 2005, World Health Organization, Article 13.

39 IHR 2005, Article 2.

40 IHR, Article 3.

41 Through section 129 of the Health and Social Care Act 2008 (a new act is sometimes used to amend an existing one, as happened here). The Explanatory Notes, a useful document which comes with an Act of Parliament to help people understand what the act is doing, says at paragraph 30 'The IHR are the means by which WHO aims to prevent and control the international spread of disease, by action that is commensurate with and restricted to public health risks, and which avoids unnecessary interference with international traffic and trade. The previous International Health Regulations (1969) were concerned with action at international borders in relation to three specific infectious diseases (cholera, plague and yellow fever), but increasingly were recognised as unable to deal with new threats, such as SARS. The new IHR are concerned with infectious diseases generally, and also with contamination . . . This Act amends the Public Health Act 1984 to

enable IHR to be implemented, including WHO recommendations issued under them.'

42 Hansard, HC Debate, 21 May 2008.

43 Earl Howe, also known as Frederick Curzon.

44 Baroness Stern.

45 Hansard, HC Debate, 15 July 2008.

46 Peter Shadbolt, 'SARS 10 years on: how dogged detective work defeated an epidemic', CNN, 21 February 2013, edition.cnn.com/2013/02/21/world/asia/sars-amoy-gardens/index.html.

47 Rory Carroll and Jo Truckman, 'Swine flu: Mexico braces for unprecedented lockdown', *Guardian*, 30 April 2009, www.theguardian.com/world/2009/apr/30/swine-flu-mexico-government-lockdown.

48 'Influenza A(H1N1): lessons learned and preparedness', World Health Organization, 2 July 2009, www.who.int/director-general/speeches/detail/influenza-a(h1n1)-lessons-learned-and-preparedness.

49 D. Stathakopoulos, 'Justinianic (Early Medieval Pandemic)', in *The Oxford Dictionary of Late Antiquity* (Oxford, 2018).

50 For more information, see Melissa de Witte, 'For Renaissance Italians, combating black plague was as much about politics as it was science, according to Stanford scholar', 12 May 2020, news.stanford.edu/2020/05/12/combating-black-plague-just-much-politics-science.

51 G. Tobyn, 'How England first managed a national infection crisis: implementation of the Plague Orders of 1578 compared with COVID-19 lockdown March to May 2020', *Social Sciences & Humanities Open*, 3:1, 2021.

52 Ibid.

53 *Orders, thought meete by her Majestie, and her privie Councell, to be executed throughout the counties of this realme, in such townes, villages and other places, as are, or may be hereafter infected with the plague, for the stay of further increase of the same* (London, 1578).

54 Rebecca Totaro, *The Plague in Print: Essential Elizabethan Sources, 1558–1603* (University Park, PA, 2010), p. 47.

55 Daniel Defoe, *A Journal of the Plague Year* (London, 1722).

56 For more information, see Eugenia Tognotti, 'Lessons from the history of quarantine, from plague to Influenza A', *Emerging Infectious Diseases*, 19:2, 2013, pp. 254–9. Available online at www.ncbi.nlm.nih.gov/pmc/articles/PMC3559034/pdf/12-0312.pdf.

57 Eugenia Tognotti, *The Asiatic Monster: History of Cholera in Italy* [in Italian] (Rome and Bari, 2000).

58 Ibid.

59 '1918 Pandemic (H1N1 virus)', Centers for Disease Control and Prevention, https://www.cdc.gov/flu/pandemic-resources/1918-pandemic-h1n1.html.

60 For more information, see Cara Downes and Simon Mitchell, 'Closed borders and broken agreements: Spanish flu in Australia', National Archives of Australia, 30 March 2021, www.naa.gov.au/blog/closed-borders-and-broken-agreements-spanish-flu-australia.

61 Laura Spinney, *Pale Rider: The Spanish Flu of 1918 and How It Changed the World* (London, 2018).

62 For more information, see Robert Hume, '"Far too little, too late": what happened when Spanish flu hit Britain?', *History Extra*, 2 March 2021, www.historyextra.com/period/first-world-war/spanish-flu-britain-how-many-died-quarantine-corona-virus-deaths-pandemic.

63 'Coronavirus: how they tried to curb Spanish flu pandemic in 1918', BBC News, 10 May 2020, www.bbc.co.uk/news/in-pictures-52564371.

64 A. W. Crosby, *America's Forgotten Pandemic: The Influenza of 1918* (Cambridge, 2003), p. 112.

65 H. Markel et al., 'Nonpharmaceutical interventions implemented by US cities during the 1918–1919 influenza pandemic', *JAMA*, 298:6, 2007, pp. 644–54.

66 Nik Martin, 'SARS remembered – how a deadly respiratory virus hit Asian economies', Deutsche Welle, 22 January 2020, www.dw.com/en/sars-remembered-how-a-deadly-respiratory-virus-hit-asian-economies/a-52088462.

67 C. Coltart et al., 'The Ebola outbreak, 2013–2016: old lessons for new epidemics', *Philosophical Transactions of the Royal Society of London B: Biological Sciences*, 372:1721, 2017.

68 For more information, see I. Rasul et al., 'What happens after the lockdown ends? Lessons from the 2015 Ebola epidemic in Sierra Leone', International Growth Centre, 25 May 2020, www.theigc.org/blog/what-happens-after-the-lockdown-ends-lessons-from-the-2015-ebola-epidemic-in-sierra-leone.

69 For a full list, see en.wikipedia.org/wiki/Ebola_virus_epidemic_in_Sierra_Leone#Travel_restrictions.

70 This was published in the *Gazette*, the rather antiquated (in the days of the internet) but still occasionally used repository for public notices: www.thegazette.co.uk/all-notices/notice?noticetypes=1717.

71 Angela Giuffrida and Lauren Cochrane, 'Italy imposes draconian rules to stop spread of coronavirus', *Guardian*, 23 February 2020, www.theguardian.com/world/2020/feb/23/italy-draconian-measures-effort-halt-coronavirus-outbreak-spread.

72 Manaugh and Twilley, p. 8.

73 Colin Packham and Renju Jose, 'Australia to use biosecurity law to restrict movements of coronavirus patients', Reuters, 3 March 2020, www.reuters.com/article/us-health-coronavirus-australia/australia-to-use-biosecurity-law-to-restrict-movements-of-coronavirus-patients-idUSKBN20Q06W.

3. Take It on the Chin

1 Heather Stewart, 'Cummings brought to life what many already knew about Johnson's failures', *Guardian*, 26 May 2021, www.theguardian.com/politics/2021/may/26/cummings-brought-to-life-what-many-already-knew-about-johnsons-failures. '[Cummings] described the prime minister's dogged refusal to listen to scientific

advice or learn the lessons of the March lockdown. He told of Johnson's repeated references to "the mayor from Jaws".'

2 'Coronavirus: woman in 70s becomes first virus fatality in UK', BBC News, 5 March 2020, www.bbc.co.uk/news/uk-51759602.

3 'Coronavirus: UK moving towards "delay" phase of virus plan as cases hit 115', BBC News, 5 March 2020, www.bbc.co.uk/news/uk-51749352.

4 'Coronavirus: Northern Italy quarantines 16 million people', BBC News, 8 March 2020, www.bbc.co.uk/news/world-middle-east-51787238.

5 'COVID-19: government announces moving out of contain phase and into delay', 12 March 2020, www.gov.uk/government/news/covid-19-government-announces-moving-out-of-contain-phase-and-into-delay.

6 'Addendum to fifteenth SAGE meeting on Covid-19, 13th March 2020', para. 24, assets.publishing.service.gov.uk/government/uploads/system/uploads/attachment_data/file/888783/S0383_Fifteenth_SAGE_meeting_on_Wuhan_Coronavirus__Covid-19__.pdf.

7 @adamwagner1 on Twitter, 15 March 2020, twitter.com/AdamWagner1/status/1239152935147311104.

8 Winston Churchill, speech delivered at the University of Zurich, 19 September 1946, rm.coe.int/16806981f3.

9 A. W. Brian Simpson, *Human Rights and the End of Empire* (Oxford, 2001), p. 605.

10 Ed Bates, *The Evolution of the European Convention on Human Rights* (Oxford, 2010), p. 58.

11 Read the full European Convention on Human Rights at www.echr.coe.int/documents/convention_eng.pdf.

12 Ibid., Article 46.

13 Jack Hanning, 'Democracy through the looking-glass', speech given to the Association of Schools of Political Studies of the Council of Europe, November 2014, www.schoolsofpoliticalstudies.eu/index.php/en/library/articles/143-democracy-through-the-looking-glass.

14 'The popularity of the Nazis', Auschwitz-Birkenau Memorial and Museum, www.auschwitz.org/en/history/before-the-extermination/the-popularity-of-the-nazis.

15 Jon Henley, 'EU brings in travel ban as France joins coronavirus lockdown', *Guardian*, 17 March 2020, www.theguardian.com/world/2020/mar/17/coronavirus-france-on-war-footing-as-europe-locks-down-macron.

16 'What the Coronavirus Bill will do', 26 March 2020, www.gov.uk/government/publications/coronavirus-bill-what-it-will-do/what-the-coronavirus-bill-will-do.

17 A new act of Parliament would probably still have been needed to give the Scottish and Northern Ireland Parliaments powers to make their own emergency public health regulations, as they were not covered by the Public Health Act.

18 *Coronavirus Act 2000 Two Years On*, House of Commons Public Administration and Constitutional Affairs Committee, Seventh Report of Session 2021–22, 18 March 2022, para. 10, committees.parliament.uk/publications/9356/documents/160933/default.

19 @Dominic2306 (Dominic Cummings) on Twitter, 3 November 2021, twitter.com/Dominic2306/status/1455912337182019587.

20 *Coronavirus Act 2000 Two Years On*, para. 52.

21 In schedules 18 and 19.

22 @Dominic2306 on Twitter, 1 August 2021, twitter.com/Dominic2306/status/1421901234596892680.

23 Kate Proctor and Vikram Dodd, '"Zero prospect" of London lockdown involving movement limits, says No 10', *Guardian*, 19 March 2020, www.theguardian.com/world/2020/mar/19/zero-prospect-of-london-lockdown-involving-movement-limits-says-no-10.

24 *Coronavirus: Lessons Learned to Date*, House of Commons Health and Social Care and Science and Technology Committees, Sixth Report of the Health and Social Care Committee and Third Report of the Science and Technology Committee of Session

2021–22, 12 October 2021, para. 77, committees.parliament.uk/publications/7496/documents/78687/default.

25 Ibid., paras. 108–9.

26 Ibid., para. 81.

27 See the section 'Partygate' in Chapter 8.

28 *Coronavirus: Lessons Learned to Date*, para. 91.

29 Chelsea Bruce-Lockhart, John Burn-Murdoch and Alex Barker, 'The shocking coronavirus study that rocked the UK and US', *Financial Times*, 19 March 2020, www.ft.com/content/16764a22-69ca-11ea-a3c9-1fe6fedcca75.

30 'Prime Minister's statement on coronavirus (COVID-19): 16 March 2020', www.gov.uk/government/speeches/pm-statement-on-coronavirus-16-march-2020.

31 'Prime Minister's statement on coronavirus (COVID-19): 18 March 2020', www.gov.uk/government/speeches/pm-statement-on-coronavirus-18-march-2020.

32 *Miller, R (On the Application Of) v The Prime Minister* [2019] UKSC 41, para. 55, www.supremecourt.uk/cases/docs/uksc-2019-0192-judgment.pdf.

4. *You Must Stay at Home*

1 Matthew d'Ancona, 'Sick man: transcript', Tortoise Media, 19 June 2020, www.tortoisemedia.com/2020/06/19/sick-man-boris-johnson-transcript.

2 My memory of this is accurate: there was not a cloud in the sky for the first week of lockdown in London. www.timeanddate.com/weather/uk/london/historic?month=3&year=2020.

3 'Prime Minister's statement on coronavirus (COVID-19): 23 March 2020', www.gov.uk/government/speeches/pm-address-to-the-nation-on-coronavirus-23-march-2020.

4 @adamwagner1 on Twitter, 24 March 2020, twitter.com/AdamWagner1/status/1242371854033092609.

5 @adamwagner1 on Twitter, 24 March 2020, twitter.com/AdamWagner1/status/1242381086816165889.

6 Jonathan Sumption, 'There is a difference between the law and official instructions', *The Times*, 26 March 2020, www.thetimes.co.uk/article/there-is-a-difference-between-the-law-and-official-instructions-j9tthqnrf.

7 At the end of 2021, I would debate Lord Sumption at the Oxford Union. I was for the motion 'This House Would Give Up Liberty for Safety'. Lord Sumption was against. Ultimately, he was quite reserved, making a rather philosophical contribution with which I largely sympathised. His teammates, anti-lockdown campaigners Professor Karol Sikora and Luke Johnson, were far more tub-thumping, with Professor Sikora dressing up in the crow-like mask of a medieval plague doctor. My side won the vote, though given the febrile atmosphere in the chamber during the speeches of the rabble-rousers on the other side, I was sure it would go the other way.

8 See, for example, Sir John Laws, 'The rule of law: the presumption of liberty and justice', *Judicial Review*, 22:4, 2017, pp. 365–73. Sir John said that the maxim is reversed for public bodies, and notably the government: everything which is not allowed is forbidden.

9 Theodoros II, 'Written in human blood: Draconian laws and the dawn of democracy', Today I Found Out, 9 January 2014, www.todayifoundout.com/index.php/2014/01/draconian-laws-written-human-blood-rather-ink.

10 Hansard, HC Debate, 4 May 2020.

11 See the useful Institute for Government explainer: 'Coronavirus and devolution', www.instituteforgovernment.org.uk/explainers/coronavirus-and-devolution.

12 'CPS announces review findings for first 200 cases under coronavirus laws', Crown Prosecution Service, 15 May 2020,

www.cps.gov.uk/cps/news/cps-announces-review-findings-first-200-cases-under-coronavirus-laws.

13 All of these were questions which were regularly debated and agonised over during that period. See, for example, Will Taylor, 'Coronavirus: "messy" lockdown advice means people don't know if they can go out to buy Easter eggs, says lawyer', Yahoo! News, 31 March 2020, www.yahoo.com/news/coronavirus-uk-lockdown-easter-150015610.html, one of the many bizarre instances throughout the pandemic when my musings on a topic on Twitter became national news.

14 Sam Smedley, 'Picking up a puppy is NOT essential travel', *News & Star*, 30 March 2020, www.newsandstar.co.uk/news/18344970.picking-puppy-not-essential-travel.

15 Jess Warren, 'Police set up roadblock to check drivers are on essential journeys', *Wokingham Today*, 1 April 2020, wokingham.today/police-set-up-roadblock-to-check-drivers-are-on-essential-journeys.

16 @DerbysPolice on Twitter, 26 March 2020, twitter.com/DerbysPolice/status/1243168931503882241.

17 Vikram Dodd and Owen Bowcott, 'Derbyshire police chief defends force's reaction to lockdown', *Guardian*, 31 March 2020, www.theguardian.com/uk-news/2020/mar/31/derbyshire-police-chief-defends-forces-reaction-to-lockdown.

18 @ChrisMasonBBC on Twitter, 31 March 2020, twitter.com/ChrisMasonBBC/status/1244873365451653121.

19 'The Health Protection (Coronavirus, Restrictions) (England) Regulations 2020', College of Policing, 26 March 2020, web.archive.org/web/20200331180752/www.college.police.uk/News/College-news/Pages/Health-Protection-Guidelines.aspx.

20 This exchange is recorded in a Twitter thread from the same day: @adamwagner1, 30 March 2020, twitter.com/AdamWagner1/status/1244634719611912192.

21 'Fixed Penalty Notices (FPNs) issued under COVID-19 emergency health regulations by police forces in England and Wales',

NPCC, 16 March 2022, cdn.prgloo.com/media/d0f7e8f380ad402ea48e70a85bc389eb.pdf.

22 'Coronavirus review findings, March–August 2021', Crown Prosecution Service, 30 September 2021, www.cps.gov.uk/cps/news/coronavirus-review-findings-march-august-2021.

23 The Prosecution of Offences Act 1985 (Specified Proceedings) (Amendment) Order 2020, (UKSI 2020/562) and The Prosecution of Offences Act 1985 (Specified Proceedings) (Coronavirus) (Amendment) Order 2021, (UKSI 2021/126). The effect of this instrument is explained in this letter from the Attorney General, 3 June 2020: committees.parliament.uk/publications/1420/documents/12931/default.

24 As diligently reported by the *Evening Standard*'s Tristan Kirk: 'London's Covid-19 rule breakers fined over £1m in closed-door courts', *Evening Standard*, 3 December 2021, www.standard.co.uk/news/crime/covid19-breach-lockdown-police-single-justice-prosecutions-one-million-b969662.html.

25 'Joint Committee on Human Rights: every Fixed Penalty Notice issued under coronavirus regulations must be reviewed', 27 April 2021, committees.parliament.uk/committee/93/human-rights-joint-committee/news/154842/joint-committee-on-human-rights-every-fixed-penalty-notice-issued-under-coronavirus-regulations-must-be-reviewed. I was Specialist Adviser to this inquiry and assisted with this report.

26 Steven Swinford, Oliver Wright and Henry Zeffman, '"Wine-time Fridays": boozy culture where Downing Street staff slept off hangovers on sofas', *The Times*, 15 January 2022, www.thetimes.co.uk/article/wine-time-fridays-boozy-culture-where-downing-street-staff-slept-off-hangovers-on-sofas-dc92hkdf5.

27 The parents of Harry Dunn, a young man who had been killed in a motorcycle accident caused by the wife of an American spy. See @RaddSeiger on Twitter, 27 March 2020, twitter.com/RaddSeiger/status/1243526627763642369.

28 Rowena Mason, 'Boris Johnson boasted of shaking hands on day Sage warned not to', *Guardian,* 5 May 2020, www.theguardian.com/politics/2020/may/05/boris-johnson-boasted-of-shaking-hands-on-day-sage-warned-not-to.

29 'Dominic Cummings scandal', Wikipedia, en.wikipedia.org/wiki/Dominic_Cummings_scandal.

30 'Dominic Cummings tells committee he didn't tell "full story" about Durham trip – but Barnard Castle drive really was to test his eyesight', Sky News, 26 May 2021, news.sky.com/story/dominic-cummings-i-didnt-tell-the-full-story-about-lockdown-durham-trip-12317511.

31 Daisy Fancourt, 'People started breaking Covid rules when they saw those with privilege ignore them', *Guardian,* 2 January 2021, www.theguardian.com/commentisfree/2021/jan/02/follow-covid-restrictions-break-rules-compliance. The COVID-19 Social Study reports can be found at www.covidsocialstudy.org/results.

32 @SuellaBraverman on Twitter, 23 May 2020, twitter.com/suellabraverman/status/1264174355975671810.

33 Alasdair Sandford, 'Half of humanity now on lockdown as 90 countries call for confinement', Euronews, 3 April 2020, www.euronews.com/2020/04/02/coronavirus-in-europe-spain-s-death-toll-hits-10-000-after-record-950-new-deaths-in-24-hou.

34 Adam Wagner, 'In a new age of emergency laws, human rights are more important than ever', *New Statesman*, 31 March 2020, www.newstatesman.com/politics/uk-politics/2020/03/emergency-laws-human-rights-pandemic-coronavirus.

35 A complaint which was summarily dismissed, I should add.

36 'Rights in the time of COVID-19: lessons from HIV for an effective, community-led response', United Nations, March 2020, www.unaids.org/sites/default/files/media_asset/human-rights-and-covid-19_en.pdf.

37 'UN Secretary-General António Guterres calls for a "ceasefire" in homes as violence against women and girls surges', Spotlight Initiative, 5 April 2020, www.spotlightinitiative.org/fr/node/18943.

38 'We must respect human rights and stand united against the coronavirus pandemic', Council of Europe, 16 March 2020, www.coe.int/en/web/commissioner/-/we-must-respect-human-rights-and-stand-united-against-the-coronavirus-pandemic.
39 Better Human Podcast, www.betterhumanpodcast.com. I recommend in particular episodes 16 and 17.
40 @WHO on Twitter, 13 October 2020, twitter.com/who/status/1316020010540625920.

5. *The Lockdown Bites*

1 @adamwagner1 on Twitter, 8 April 2020, twitter.com/AdamWagner1/status/1247902767366017027.
2 @CambridgeCops on Twitter, 10 April 2020, twitter.com/CambridgeCops/status/1248546787394293760.
3 Adam Wagner, 'Why policing the coronavirus lockdown is an impossible task – that will lead to wrongful convictions', 10 April 2020, *Daily Telegraph*, www.telegraph.co.uk/news/2020/04/10/policing-coronavirus-lockdown-impossible-task-will-lead-wrongful.
4 @adamwagner1 on Twitter, 15 April 2020, twitter.com/AdamWagner1/status/1250442453024309250.
5 Article 2 of the First Protocol to the ECHR: 'No person shall be denied the right to education. In the exercise of any functions which it assumes in relation to education and to teaching, the State shall respect the right of parents to ensure such education and teaching in conformity with their own religious and philosophical convictions.'
6 Along with my colleague Caoilfhionn Gallagher QC.
7 The full letter, dated 9 April 2020, can be read here: www.dropbox.com/s/2gscecp99josicz/GLPtoGavinWilliamson.pdf?dl=0.
8 By the Institute for Public Policy Research in their March 2020 report, 'Children of the pandemic': see www.ippr.org/files/2020-03/1585586431_children-of-the-pandemic.pdf.

9 'Hundreds of thousands more laptops to support disadvantaged pupils learn at home', Department for Education, 12 January 2021, www.gov.uk/government/news/hundreds-of-thousands-more-laptops-to-support-disadvantaged-pupils-learn-at-home.

10 See my Twitter thread: @adamwagner1, 20 April 2020, twitter.com/AdamWagner1/status/1252251092412497920.

11 The Health Protection (Coronavirus, Restrictions) (England) (Amendment) Regulations 2020, UKSI 2020/447.

12 The Health Protection (Coronavirus, Restrictions) (England) (Amendment) (No. 2) Regulations 2020, UKSI 2020/500.

13 'Drivers of the higher COVID-19 incidence, morbidity and mortality among minority ethnic groups', SAGE, 23 September 2020 (updated 20 May 2022), https://www.gov.uk/government/publications/drivers-of-the-higher-covid-19-incidence-morbidity-and-mortality-among-minority-ethnic-groups-23-september-2020.

14 R. W. Aldridge et al., 'Black, Asian and minority ethnic groups in England are at increased risk of death from COVID-19: indirect standardisation of NHS mortality data', *Wellcome Open Research*, 5:88, 2020. Retrieved from wellcomeopenresearch.org/articles/5-88.

15 Zubaida Haque, Laia Becares and Nick Treloar, 'Over-exposed and under-protected: the devastating impact of COVID-19 on Black and minority ethnic communities in Great Britain', Runnymede Trust, 2020. Available at www.runnymedetrust.org/publications/over-exposed-and-under-protected.

16 F. Mahmood et al., 'Impact of COVID-19 pandemic on ethnic minority communities: a qualitative study on the perspectives of ethnic minority community leaders', *BMJ Open*, 11, 2021.

17 Public Health England, 'Beyond the data: understanding the impact of COVID-19 on BAME groups', June 2020, assets.publishing.service.gov.uk/government/uploads/system/uploads/

attachment_data/file/892376/COVID_stakeholder_engagement_synthesis_beyond_the_data.pdf.

18 Mirren Gidda, 'Revealed: surge in police use of force during height of lockdown', Liberty Investigates, 29 October 2020, libertyinvestigates.org.uk/articles/revealed-surge-in-police-use-of-force-during-height-of-lockdown.

19 Scarlet Harris et al., 'A threat to public safety: policing, racism and the Covid-19 pandemic', Institute of Race Relations, 2021. Available at irr.org.uk/wp-content/uploads/2021/09/A-threat-to-public-safety-v3.pdf.

20 The Health Protection (Coronavirus, Restrictions) (England) (Amendment) (No. 3) Regulations 2020, UKSI 2020/558.

21 Catriona Harvey-Jenner, 'Sex is now illegal in the UK between people who don't live together', 1 June 2020, www.cosmopolitan.com/uk/reports/a32729254/sex-illegal-people-different-house holds.

22 The Health Protection (Coronavirus, Restrictions) (England) (Amendment) (No. 4) Regulations 2020, UKSI 2020/588.

23 For more on this, see my Twitter thread on the topic: @adamwagner1, 7 February 2021, twitter.com/AdamWagner1/status/1358463275063779329.

24 @adamwagner1 on Twitter, 23 September 2020, twitter.com/AdamWagner1/status/1308793043349372932.

25 For example, my understanding is that in the 2021 lockdown Germany had a curfew from 8 p.m. to 5 a.m. but allowed one external person into the house. France had a 6 p.m. to 6 a.m. curfew. See @adamwagner1 on Twitter, 7 February 2021, twitter.com/AdamWagner1/status/1358527784449105920.

26 See the article by my colleague Susie Alegre, 'Squeamish ministers must include casual sex exemption in lockdown roadmap', *City A.M.*, 23 February 2021, www.cityam.com/squeamish-ministers-must-include-casual-sex-exemption-in-lockdown-roadmap.

27 Emma Harrison, 'Matt Hancock quits as health secretary after breaking social distance guidance', BBC News, 27 June 2021, www.bbc.co.uk/news/uk-57625508.
28 Justin Parkinson, 'Matt Hancock affair: health secretary apologises for breaking social distancing guidelines', BBC News, 25 June 2021, www.bbc.co.uk/news/uk-politics-57612441.
29 This was how it was referred to in another Metropolitan Police policy, Gold Strategy Op Pima, authored by DAC Jane Connors, who would take the lead in the Partygate investigation. The Op Pima policy was revealed as part of the police disclosure in the #ReclaimTheseStreets case, which I discuss in Chapter 8.

6. Patchwork Summer

1 The Health Protection (Coronavirus, International Travel) (England) Regulations 2020, UKSI 2020/568.
2 The Health Protection (Coronavirus, Wearing of Face Coverings on Public Transport) (England) Regulations 2020, UKSI 2020/592.
3 'Transmission of SARS-CoV-2 and Mitigating Measures, EMG-SAGE', 4 June 2020, assets.publishing.service.gov.uk/government/uploads/system/uploads/attachment_data/file/892043/S0484_Transmission_of_SARS-CoV-2_and_Mitigating_Measures.pdf.
4 Becky Little, 'When mask-wearing rules in the 1918 pandemic faced resistance', *History*, 6 May 2020, www.history.com/news/1918-spanish-flu-mask-wearing-resistance.
5 Hansard, HC Debate, 6 July 2020.
6 Tom Hickman, 'Eight ways to reinforce and revise the lockdown law', UK Constitutional Law Association, 16 April 2020, ukconstitutionallaw.org/2020/04/16/tom-hickman-eight-ways-to-reinforce-and-revise-the-lockdown-law. See also a range of other articles written by Tom, such as 'The use and misuse of guidance during the UK's coronavirus lockdown', SSRN, 4 September 2020, ssrn.com/abstract=368657.

7 Adam Wagner, 'Can we make good laws during a bad pandemic?', *Prospect*, 16 April 2020, www.prospectmagazine.co.uk/politics/coronavirus-covid-19-law-parliament-emergency-powers.
8 The Health Protection (Coronavirus, Restrictions) (Leicester) Regulations 2020, UKSI 2020/685.
9 Fiona Hamilton and John Simpson, 'Police will turn back drivers fleeing Leicester's coronavirus lockdown', *The Times*, 1 July 2020, www.thetimes.co.uk/article/police-will-turn-back-drivers-fleeing-leicester-s-coronavirus-lockdown-pml20c785.
10 @adamwagner1 on Twitter, 1 July 2020, twitter.com/AdamWagner1/status/1278241218435133441.
11 Sandish Shoker, 'Leicester Muslims mark second Eid of extended lockdown', BBC News, 1 August 2020, www.bbc.co.uk/news/uk-england-leicestershire-53585829.
12 The Health Protection (Coronavirus, Restrictions) (Blackburn with Darwen and Luton) Regulations 2020, UKSI 2020/800.
13 The Health Protection (Coronavirus, Restrictions on Gatherings) (North of England) Regulations 2020, UKSI 2020/828.
14 The Health Protection (Coronavirus, Restrictions) (Greencore) Regulations 2020, UKSI 2020/921.
15 The Health Protection (Coronavirus, Restrictions) (Blackburn with Darwen and Bradford) (Amendment) (No. 3) Regulations 2020, UKSI 2020/935.
16 The Health Protection (Coronavirus, Restrictions) (Bolton) Regulations 2020, UKSI 2020/974.
17 The Health Protection (Coronavirus, Restrictions) (Birmingham, Sandwell and Solihull) Regulations 2020, UKSI 2020/988.
18 The Health Protection (Coronavirus, Restrictions) (North East of England) Regulations 2020, UKSI 2020/1010.
19 'Get a discount with the Eat Out to Help Out scheme', first published 15 July 2020, www.gov.uk/guidance/get-a-discount-with-the-eat-out-to-help-out-scheme.

20 Health Protection (Coronavirus) (Restrictions on Holding of Gatherings and Amendment) (England) Regulations 2020, UKSI 2020/907.

21 Damien Gayle, 'Piers Corbyn fined £10,000 for organising anti-lockdown rally', *Guardian*, www.theguardian.com/world/2020/aug/30/piers-corbyn-fined-10000-for-organising-anti-lockdown-rally.

22 I have managed to ensure that this excellent paragraph appears in two recent judgments, *The Secretary of State for Transport & Anor v Cuciurean* [2020] EWHC 2723 at para. 50, and *The Secretary of State for Transport & Anor v Cuciurean* [2022] EWCA Civ 661 at para. 51. For this I must thank the indomitable Felicity Gerry QC, who led me in the case of *R v Jogee*, where I first came across the expression.

23 Protected by Article 7 of the European Convention on Human Rights.

24 *Hashman and Harrup v UK* [1999] 30 EHRR 241.

25 There were well over one hundred regulations restricting our behaviour from 26 March 2020 to 18 March 2022, so more than one per week on average.

26 See my Twitter thread: @adamwagner1, 6 September 2020, twitter.com/AdamWagner1/status/1302526518506201088.

27 John Stuart Mill, *On Liberty* (London, 1859; 1974), p. 68.

28 Steven Morris, 'Almost 5,000 Covid cases linked to Cornish music and surf festival', *Guardian*, 23 August 2021, www.theguardian.com/uk-news/2021/aug/23/almost-5000-covid-cases-linked-to-cornish-music-and-surf-festival-boardmasters.

29 Mill, pp. 79–80.

7. The Darkest Winter

1 The Health Protection (Coronavirus, Restrictions) (No. 2) (England) (Amendment) (No. 4) Regulations 2020, UKSI 2020/986.

2 Saffron Otter, 'Priti Patel gives definition of "mingling" that could see people fined', *Manchester Evening News*, 15 September 2020, www.manchestereveningnews.co.uk/news/uk-news/priti-patel-gives-definition-mingling-18936296.

3 *Parliamentary Scrutiny of the Government's Handling of Covid-19*, House of Commons Public Administration and Constitutional Affairs Committee, Fourth Report of Session 2019–2021, 10 September 2020, committees.parliament.uk/publications/2459/documents/24384/default.

4 *The Government's Response to COVID-19: Human Rights Implications*, Joint Committee on Human Rights, 21 September 2020, committees.parliament.uk/publications/2649/documents/26914/default. The JCHR is a cross-Parliamentary and cross-party committee chaired by Harriet Harman MP. Harman texted me out of the blue in March 2020 to see if I would be interested in advising on the new inquiry. I became one of the only lawyers in the UK who effectively had a standing brief to examine the human rights implications of the extraordinary events as they unfolded around us.

5 Daisy Fancourt et al., 'Covid-19 Social Study Results Release 17'. The accompanying media release stated: 'The general drop-off in understanding could be due to unclear messaging from the government, or a reduction in interest and engagement from people, especially with the cessation of the daily Downing Street coronavirus briefing in late June.'

6 Paul Waugh, 'Grouse shooting and hunting exempt from Johnson's "rule of six" Covid curbs', *Huffington Post*, 14 September 2020, www.huffingtonpost.co.uk/entry/boris-johnson-rule-of-six-hunting-shooting-exemption_uk_5f5f4a0c5b6b48508031 10f.

7 @Dominic2306 on Twitter, 11 May 2022, twitter.com/Dominic2306/status/1524381236667588610.

8 See www.transparency.org.

9 See 'Cabinet committees', Institute for Government, www.instituteforgovernment.org.uk/explainers/cabinet-committees.

10 @Dominic2306 on Twitter, 11 May 2022. This story had, in fact, already been reported by the *Byline Times*, though not that deals were negotiated directly by the Prime Minister.

11 Brian Cathcart, 'Government refuses to reveal taxpayer cost of secret COVID subsidy for its wealthy press friends', *Byline Times*, 8 March 2022, bylinetimes.com/2022/03/08/government-refuses-to-reveal-taxpayer-cost-of-secret-covid-subsidy-for-its-wealthy-press-friends.

12 'Investigation into the management of PPE contracts', National Audit Office, 30 March 2022, www.nao.org.uk/report/investigation-into-the-management-of-ppe-contracts.

13 Felicity Lawrence, 'Pressure on Hancock over pub landlord's Covid deal', *Guardian*, 1 December 2021, www.theguardian.com/politics/2021/dec/01/matt-hancock-says-labours-covid-contract-claims-rubbish.

14 'The PPE fiasco', Good Law Project, goodlawproject.org/case/procurement-case.

15 Nicholas Barrett and Anthony Reuben, 'Covid: why were the government's Covid contracts challenged?', BBC News, 18 January 2022, www.bbc.co.uk/news/56174954.

16 For example, *The Good Law Project, R (On the Application Of) v Minister for the Cabinet Office* [2022] EWCA Civ 21, www.bailii.org/ew/cases/EWCA/Civ/2022/21.html.

17 The Health Protection (Coronavirus, Restrictions) (Obligations of Hospitality Undertakings) (England) Regulations 2020, UKSI 2020/1008.

18 The Health Protection (Coronavirus, Restrictions) (Self-Isolation) (England) Regulations 2020, UKSI 2020/1045.

19 'Coronavirus: police granted access to details of people told to self-isolate by Test and Trace', Sky News, 18 October 2020, news.sky.com/story/coronavirus-police-granted-access-to-details-of-people-told-to-self-isolate-by-test-and-trace-12106988.

20 The Health Protection (Coronavirus, Restrictions) (Protected Areas and Linked Childcare Households) (Amendment) Regulations 2020, UKSI 2020/1019.

21 @adamwagner1 on Twitter, 30 September 2020, twitter.com/AdamWagner1/status/1311083297313902592.

22 Francis Elliott, 'Coronavirus: Rishi Sunak demanded clearer rules for lockdowns in cabinet clash', *The Times*, 8 October 2020, www.thetimes.co.uk/article/rishi-sunak-demanded-clearer-rules-for-lockdowns-in-cabinet-clash-t6dg5jr9w.

23 The Health Protection (Coronavirus, Local COVID-19 Alert Level) (Medium) (England) Regulations 2020, UKSI 2020/1103; The Health Protection (Coronavirus, Local COVID-19 Alert Level) (High) (England) Regulations 2020, UKSI 2020/1104; and The Health Protection (Coronavirus, Local COVID-19 Alert Level) (Very High) (England) Regulations 2020, UKSI 2020/1105.

24 'Statement from the mayor following talks with the government on Tier 3 restrictions', Greater Manchester Combined Authority, 20 October 2020, www.greatermanchester-ca.gov.uk/news/statement-from-the-mayor-following-talks-with-the-government-on-tier-3-restrictions.

25 The Health Protection (Coronavirus, Restrictions) (England) (No. 4) Regulations 2020, UKSI 2020/1200.

26 Ashley Cowburn, 'Coronavirus: Priti Patel bans demonstrations during England's lockdown', *Independent*, 3 November 2020, www.independent.co.uk/news/uk/politics/priti-patel-protests-england-lockdown-home-office-demonstrations-b1556584.html.

27 Heather Stewart, Josh Halliday and Helen Pidd, 'Keir Starmer urges PM to impose "circuit breaker" lockdown on England', *Guardian*, 13 October 2020, www.theguardian.com/world/2020/oct/13/keir-starmer-urges-pm-to-impose-circuit-breaker-lockdown-on-england.

28 Due, I think, to a calculating error on the part of the government, it ended up lasting twenty-seven days.

29 Lord Sumption, 'Our lives belong to us, not the state. It's morally wrong for government control freaks to tell us what we can do at Christmas', *Daily Mail*, 21 November 2020, www.dailymail.co.uk/debate/article-8973529/LORD-SUMPTION-morally-wrong-government-control-freaks-tell-Christmas.html.

30 The document is: 'Options for increasing adherence to social distancing measures', paper prepared by the behavioural science group, SPI-B, for the Scientific Advisory Group for Emergencies (SAGE), 22 March 2020, www.assets.publishing.service.gov.uk/government/uploads/system/uploads/attachment_data/file/887467/25-options-for-increasing-adherence-to-social-distancing-measures-22032020.pdf.

31 See, for example: Laura Dodsworth, 'The metrics of fear', *The Critic*, 28 September 2020, thecritic.co.uk/the-metrics-of-fear'; @ClarkeMicah (Peter Hitchens) on Twitter, 15 August 2020, twitter.com/clarkemicah/status/1294600499174477824; @SteveBakerHW (Steve Baker MP) on Twitter – also using the hashtag #1984, 28 September 2020, twitter.com/stevebakerhw/status/1310497885436497920.

32 Deaths within 28 days of positive test, coronavirus.data.gov.uk/details/deaths?areaType=overview&areaName=United%20Kingdom.

33 The Health Protection (Coronavirus, Restrictions) (All Tiers) (England) Regulations 2020, UKSI 2020/1374.

34 Jessica Elgot, Peter Walker and Rajeev Syal, 'Labour to abstain in vote on Covid tiers as Tories threaten to rebel', *Guardian*, 30 November 2020, www.theguardian.com/world/2020/nov/30/labour-to-abstain-in-vote-on-covid-tiers-as-tories-threaten-to-rebel.

35 'Coronavirus: Tory revolt brewing over "appalling" tiers plan', BBC News, 26 November 2020, www.bbc.co.uk/news/uk-politics-55087747.

36 Keep Britain Free website, www.keepbritainfree.com/mission-vision.

37 Francis Hoar, 'A disproportionate interference with rights and freedoms: the coronavirus regulations and the European Convention on Human Rights', 21 April 2020, fieldcourt.co.uk/wp-content/uploads/Francis-Hoar-Coronavirus-article-on-ECHR-compatibility-20.4.2020-2.pdf.

38 *Dolan & Ors, R (On the Application Of) v The Secretary of State for Health and Social Care & Anor* [2020] EWCA Civ 1605, www.bailii.org/ew/cases/EWCA/Civ/2020/1605.html.

39 @DimitriosGian (Dimitrios Giannoulopoulos) on Twitter, 21 July 2020, twitter.com/DimitriosGian/status/1285609580425355265.

40 'Johnson defies calls to "cancel Christmas", urging small gatherings', *Financial Times*, 16 December 2020, www.ft.com/content/39325afc-90e0-40fd-92e3-69a03063ad76.

41 The Health Protection (Coronavirus, Restrictions) (All Tiers) (England) (Amendment) Regulations 2020, UKSI 2020/1533.

42 The Health Protection (Coronavirus, Restrictions) (All Tiers and Obligations of Undertakings) (England) (Amendment) Regulations 2020, UKSI 2020/1611.

43 The Health Protection (Coronavirus, Restrictions) (No. 3) and (All Tiers) (England) (Amendment) Regulations 2021, UKSI 2021/8.

44 Better Human Podcast on YouTube, www.youtube.com/c/betterhumanpodcast.

45 I did not verify the replies; however, I did seek out information by private message which led me to the belief that the individuals were all police officers.

46 @HarrietHarman on Twitter, 24 February 2021, twitter.com/HarrietHarman/status/1364617578161860613.

47 'Fixed Penalty Notices (FPNs) issued under COVID-19 emergency health regulations by police forces in England and Wales', NPCC, 16 March 2022, cdn.prgloo.com/media/d0f7e8f380ad402ea48e70a85bc389eb.pdf.

48 Johann Foucault, 'Covid-19: plus de 760,000 amendes dressées depuis le début du confinement', Actu.fr, 16 April 2020.

49 'Spanish govt returns fines for breaking virus lockdown rules', *U.S. News*, 22 October 2021, www.usnews.com/news/world/articles/2021-10-22/spanish-govt-returns-fines-for-breaking-virus-lockdown-rules.

50 'Covid: Spain's top court rules lockdown unconstitutional', BBC News, 14 July 2021, www.bbc.co.uk/news/world-europe-57838615. Interestingly, the case was brought by the country's far-right party.

51 Italian government website, www.interno.gov.it/it/coronavirus-i-dati-dei-servizi-controllo.

52 Stephen Reicher and John Drury, 'Pandemic fatigue? How adherence to covid-19 regulations has been misrepresented and why it matters', *British Medical Journal*, 7 January 2021, blogs.bmj.com/bmj/2021/01/07/pandemic-fatigue-how-adherence-to-covid-19-regulations-has-been-misrepresented-and-why-it-matters.

53 coronavirus.data.gov.uk/details/deaths?areaType=overview&areaName=United%20Kingdom.

54 'Mitigations to Reduce Transmission of the new variant SARS-CoV-2 virus, SAGE-EMG, SPI-B, Transmission Group', 23 December 2020, https://assets.publishing.service.gov.uk/government/uploads/system/uploads/attachment_data/file/948607/s0995-mitigations-to-reduce-transmission-of-the-new-variant.pdf.

55 'Asylum seeker at Napier Barracks obtains court injunction that he must be re-housed', Deighton Pierce Glynn, 2 February 2021, dpglaw.co.uk/asylum-seeker-at-napier-barracks-obtains-court-injunction-that-he-must-be-re-housed. The barrister responsible for obtaining this order was my Doughty Street colleague Leonie Hirst.

56 *NB & Ors, R (On the Application Of) v The Secretary of State for the Home Department* [2021] EWHC 1489 (Admin).

57 Rachel Hall, Damien Gayle and Ben Quinn, 'Manchester students pull down lockdown fences around halls of residence', *Guardian*, 5 November 2020, www.theguardian.com/education/2020/nov/05/security-fence-manchester-university-student-flats.

58 I recorded a podcast on the issue – Better Human Podcast episode 32 – which you can listen to here: podcasts.apple.com/gb/podcast/better-human-podcast/id1481010283?i=1000486910691.

59 Michael Boniface, 'Hampstead protest defending Uighur Muslims takes to Volkswagen Finchley Road', *Ham & High*, 14 December 2020, www.hamhigh.co.uk/news/hampstead-uighur-muslim-pro test-in-finchley-road-volkswagen-6746978.

60 @adamwagner1 on Twitter, 2 February 2021, twitter.com/Adam Wagner1/status/1356685106740682754.

61 Rory Tingle, 'London mayor candidate Brian Rose is fined £200 for breaking lockdown rules while recording campaign video after taking to capital's streets in battle bus as he accuses Boris Johnson of "undermining democracy" ', *Daily Mail*, 25 January 2021, www.dailymail.co.uk/news/article-9184367/London-mayor-candidate-Brian-Rose-fined-200-breaking-lockdown-rules.html.

62 Human Rights Act 1998, section 6(1): 'It is unlawful for a public authority to act in a way which is incompatible with a Convention right.'

63 Charles Hymas and Christopher Hope, 'Cabinet to back guarded hotel quarantine', *Daily Telegraph*, 23 January 2021.

64 The Health Protection (Coronavirus, International Travel) (England) (Amendment) (No. 7) Regulations 2021, UKSI 2021/150.

65 Hansard, HL Debate, 22 March 2021.

66 Maeve Campbell, ' "It was like living in a cage": UK quarantine hotel reviews from former guests', Euronews.com, 1 December 2021, www.euronews.com/travel/2021/12/01/it-was-like-living-in-a-cage-uk-quarantine-hotel-reviews-from-former-guests; Robert Dex, 'Travellers stuck in £1,750 London quarantine hotel complain about "nightmare" conditions', *Evening Standard*, 24 June 2021, www.standard.co.uk/news/london/travellers-quarantine-hotel-complain-bad-food-conditions-b942501.html; 'Covid: man takes legal action over quarantine hotel stay', BBC News, 18 August 2021, www.bbc.co.uk/news/uk-england-hampshire-58257853.

67 Sue Mitchell and Sarah McDermott, 'Covid quarantine hotels: women say they were sexually harassed by guards', BBC News, 26 June 2021, www.bbc.co.uk/news/stories-57609164.

68 I worked on hotel quarantine cases with Theodora Middleton and Patrick Ormerod of Bindmans LLP, both superb, committed solicitors who acted in many successful cases over the course of the pandemic.

69 The interview on BBC Radio 4's *Today* Programme is reproduced here: @adamwagner1 on Twitter, 18 May 2021, twitter.com/AdamWagner1/status/1394662377778556932.

70 I worked on the case with Patrick Ormerod and Grace Benton of Bindmans LLP and my Doughty Street colleague Caoilfhionn Gallagher QC.

71 Led by Tom Hickman QC, with Cian Murphy and PGMBM solicitors.

72 'Hardship arrangements for those unable to pay for managed quarantine or testing', 25 September 2021. www.gov.uk/guidance/hardship-arrangements-for-those-unable-to-pay-for-managed-quarantine-or-testing.

73 *Hotta & Ors, R (On the Application Of) v The Secretary of State for Health and Social Care & Anor* [2021] EWHC 3359 (Admin), Mr Justice Fordham.

74 @adamwagner1 on Twitter, 3 August 2021, twitter.com/AdamWagner1/status/1422667471195185161.

75 All travel restrictions were revoked by The Health Protection (Coronavirus, International Travel and Operator Liability) (Revocation) (England) Regulations 2022, UKSI 2022/317, meaning that for hotel quarantine to be resurrected there would need to be new regulations, but all countries were removed from the red list on 15 December 2021.

76 'Weekly statistics for NHS Test and Trace (England), 6 January 2022 to 12 January 2022', UK Health Security Agency, 20 January 2022, p. 40, assets.publishing.service.gov.uk/government/

uploads/system/uploads/attachment_data/file/1048603/NHS_Test_and_Trace_20220120.pdf.

8. Step by Step

1 'PM statement at coronavirus press conference: 22 February 2021', www.gov.uk/government/speeches/pm-statement-at-coronavirus-press-conference-22-february-2021.

2 The Health Protection (Coronavirus, Restrictions) (Entry to Venues and Events) (England) Regulations 2021, UKSI 2021/1416.

3 'German call to ban "Jewish star" at Covid demos', BBC News, 7 May 2021, www.bbc.com/news/world-europe-57020697.

4 There is a good debunking article on this topic on the Full Fact website: Pippa Allen-Kinross, 'Why is the Nuremberg Code being used to oppose Covid-19 vaccines?', 13 May 2021, fullfact.org/health/nuremberg-code-covid.

5 In the sense that if you do not have COVID-19 you cannot transmit it. See Anika Singanayagam et al., 'Community transmission and viral load kinetics of the SARS-CoV-2 delta (B.1.617.2) variant in vaccinated and unvaccinated individuals in the UK: a prospective, longitudinal, cohort study', *Lancet Infectious Diseases*, 22:2, 2022, pp. 183–95, www.thelancet.com/journals/laninf/article/PIIS1473-3099(21)00648-4/fulltext.

6 This is a genuine and widely dispersed conspiracy theory. See Jack Goodman and Flora Carmichael, 'Coronavirus: Bill Gates "microchip" conspiracy theory and other vaccine claims fact-checked', BBC News, 30 May 2020, www.bbc.co.uk/news/52847648.

7 Adam Wagner, 'Are vaccine passports a threat to human rights?', *New Statesman*, 7 April 2021, www.newstatesman.com/politics/uk-politics/2021/04/are-vaccine-passports-threat-human-rights. See also my Better Human Podcast discussion at www.patreon.com/posts/49063332.

8 'NHS pay-rise demo organiser fined £10,000 in Manchester', BBC News, 7 March 2021, www.bbc.co.uk/news/uk-england-manchester-56312817. The FPN was eventually rescinded (reported on 25 May 2022) following the work of Bindmans LLP and my colleague Jude Bunting: www.bindmans.com/news/nhs-nurses-win-compensation-claim-against-police-following-covid-fine.

9 @adamwagner1 on Twitter, 7 March 2021, twitter.com/AdamWagner1/status/1368615258340945921.

10 John Halford, Theodora Middleton and Patrick Ormerod of Bindmans LLP, and barristers Tom Hickman QC and Pippa Woodrow.

11 *Leigh & Ors v Commissioner of the Police of the Metropolis & Anor* [2021] EWHC 661 (Admin).

12 Jessica Leigh, Anna Birley, Henna Shah and Jamie Klingler.

13 *Leigh & Ors v The Commissioner of Police of the Metropolis* [2022] EWHC 527 (Admin).

14 Prime Minister in the House of Commons on 30 June 2021, https://www.theyworkforyou.com/debates/?id=2021-06-30b.256.0.

15 The Health Protection (Coronavirus, Restrictions) (Steps etc.) (England) (Revocation and Amendment) Regulations 2021, UKSI 2021/848.

16 Glen Owen, 'Boris Johnson cancels plans for Churchillian Freedom Day launch – after No 10 alarm over a surge in infections', *Daily Mail*, 17 July 2021, www.dailymail.co.uk/news/article-9798757/Boris-Johnson-cancels-plans-Churchillian-Freedom-Day-launch.html.

17 @tnewtondunn (Tom Newton Dunn) on Twitter, 18 July 2021, twitter.com/tnewtondunn/status/1416695145693683714.

18 The Health Protection (Coronavirus, International Travel and Operator Liability) (England) (Amendment) (No. 19) Regulations 2021, UKSI 2021/1323; The Health Protection (Coronavirus, International Travel and Operator Liability) (England) (Amendment) (No. 20) Regulations 2021, UKSI 2021/1331.

19 The Health Protection (Coronavirus, Wearing of Face Coverings) (England) (Amendment) Regulations 2021, UKSI 2021/1400.

20 The Health Protection (Coronavirus, Restrictions) (Entry to Venues and Events) (England) Regulations 2021, UKSI/1416.

21 'Omicron restrictions take effect', Scottish Government, 27 December 2021, www.gov.scot/news/omicron-restrictions-take-effect.

22 The term was in a sense misleading because the self-isolation regulations did not require a person to self-isolate if they were 'pinged' by the NHS COVID app – only, generally, if notified by NHS Test and Trace. But the guidance was for people to isolate whether or not they had been notified, i.e. if they had a positive lateral flow test but hadn't followed it up with a PCR, therefore not notifying the NHS.

23 *Francis, R (On the Application Of) v The Secretary of State for Health And Social Care* [2020] EWHC 3287, para. 63.

24 As quoted in Sue Gray, 'Findings of Second Permanent Secretary's investigation into alleged gatherings on government premises during Covid restrictions', 25 May 2022, assets.publishing.service.gov.uk/government/uploads/system/uploads/attachment_data/file/1078404/2022-05-25_FINAL_FINDINGS_OF_SECOND_PERMANENT_SECRETARY_INTO_ALLEGED_GATHERINGS.pdf.

25 Pippa Crerar, 'Boris Johnson "broke Covid lockdown rules" with Downing Street parties at Xmas', *Daily Mirror*, 30 November 2021, www.mirror.co.uk/news/politics/boris-johnson-broke-covid-lockdown-25585238.

26 'Downing Street staff shown joking in leaked recording about Christmas party they later denied', ITV News, 10 December 2021, www.itv.com/news/2021-12-07/no-10-staff-joke-in-leaked-recording-about-christmas-party-they-later-denied.

27 I was led by Danny Friedman QC and instructed by Jamie Potter and Helen Fry of Bindmans LLP.

28 Laura Kuenssberg, 'Partygate: insiders tell of packed No 10 lockdown parties', BBC News, 24 May 2022, www.bbc.co.uk/news/uk-politics-61566410.

9. Freedom Regained?

1 The Health Protection (Coronavirus, International Travel and Operator Liability) (Revocation) (England) Regulations 2022, UKSI 2022/317.
2 Simiao Chen et al., 'Fangcang shelter hospitals: a novel concept for responding to public health emergencies', *Lancet*, 395:10232, 2020, pp. 1305–14, www.thelancet.com/journals/lancet/article/PIIS0140-6736(20)30744-3/fulltext.
3 Aristotle in his *Poetics*.
4 Iain Martin, 'No one fears Boris Johnson, and that's a problem', *The Times*, 25 May 2022, www.thetimes.co.uk/article/no-one-fears-boris-johnson-and-thats-a-problem-7fsvkv2tt.
5 Pablo G. Hidalgo, Fiona de Londras and Daniella Lock, 'Parliamentary scrutiny of extending emergency measures in the two Scottish Coronavirus Acts: on the question of timing', UK Constitutional Law Blog, 21 June 2021, as quoted in Joelle Grogan and Alice Donald (eds.), *Routledge Handbook of Law and the COVID-19 Pandemic* (Abingdon, 2022), Chapter 5.
6 Ibid., Chapter 16.
7 John Scott QC and John Wadham respectively.
8 I and Eleanor Hourigan, Counsel to the Joint Committee on Human Rights, met with the two Johns on an informal, semi-regular basis to compare notes about the different jurisdictions, meetings at which we generally goggled at the extraordinary events unfolding around us and discussed how policing was working across the UK. But this was no substitute for an independent reviewer.

9 Alastair McLellan and Kamran Abbasi, 'The NHS is not living with covid, it's dying from it', *Health Service Journal*, 18 July 2022, www.hsj.co.uk/coronavirus/the-nhs-is-not-living-with-covid-its-dying-from-it/7032824.article.

10 'Reverend Dr William J U Philip and others for judicial review of the closure of places of worship in Scotland [2021] ScotCS CSOH_32', www.bailii.org/scot/cases/ScotCS/2021/2021_CSOH_32.html. The complete ban on public and private worship in Scotland was unconstitutional and a breach of Article 9 of the ECHR (the right to freedom to manifest religion).

11 Johns Hopkins University, Coronavirus Resource Center, https://coronavirus.jhu.edu/data/mortality.

12 'Democracy Denied? The urgent need to rebalance power between Parliament and the Executive', Delegated Powers and Regulatory Reform Committee, 24 November 2021, https://committees.parliament.uk/publications/7960/documents/82286/default/.

General Index

Index of Legislation

Primary legislation

Secondary legislation

Index of Cases